EVERYTHING YOU NEED TO KNOW ABOUT SAVING ENERGY:

—How planting trees can help cut down your energy consumption.

—How you can cool your house without air conditioning.

—How much power each of your home appliances uses.

—How inexpensive fixtures can lower your hot water bills.

—The ways in which solar heating can be a money-saving reality in your home, garage, or pool.

—How to get more heat from your fireplace.

—Where to go for the equipment and aid you need in converting your home energy plant.

—And a great many things you have probably never realized that can keep your house from becoming a drain on your bank account while permanently increasing its resale value.

The Energy-Efficient Home:
A MANUAL FOR SAVING FUEL AND USING SOLAR, WOOD, AND WIND POWER

"Very practical . . . provides concrete guidance for saving fuel and for using renewable energy." —René Dubos

STEVEN ROBINSON, specializes in energy-efficient architecture. His practice includes residential, institutional and commercial design. He serves as a consultant on the Residential Solar Heating and Cooling Demonstration Program sponsored by the Department of Housing and Urban Development.

FRED S. DUBIN, President of Dubin-Bloome Associates, is a consulting engineer with a wide experience in total building design. He is the author of the recently published "Energy Conservation in New and Existing Buildings", a technical manual for industrial and commercial applications. He is a consultant to the Department of Energy and H.U.D. for solar energy and energy conservation.

THE ENERGY EFFICIENT HOME

A MANUAL FOR SAVING FUEL AND USING SOLAR, WOOD, AND WIND POWER

By Steven Robinson with Fred S. Dubin

and the assistance of Pamela Belyea

Illustrations by James A. Victorine

A PLUME BOOK
NEW AMERICAN LIBRARY

TIMES MIRROR
NEW YORK, LONDON AND SCARBOROUGH, ONTARIO

PLUME TRADEMARK REG. U.S. PAT. OFF. AND FOREIGN COUNTRIES
REGISTERED TRADEMARK—MARCA REGISTRADA
HECHO EN FORGE VILLAGE, MASS., U.S.A.

SIGNET, SIGNET CLASSICS, MENTOR, PLUME and
MERIDIAN BOOKS are published
in the United States by
The New American Library, Inc.,
1301 Avenue of the Americas, New York,
New York 10019, in Canada by
The New American Library of Canada Limited,
81 Mack Avenue, Scarborough,
Ontario M1L 1M8, in the United Kingdom by
The New English Library Limited,
Barnard's Inn, Holborn, London,
E.C. 1, England.

First Plume Printing, October, 1978
1 2 3 4 5 6 7 8 9

PRINTED IN THE UNITED STATES OF AMERICA

For my Father
A man of vision,
compassion, and immense simple dignity

ACKNOWLEDGMENTS

This book greatly benefited from family and friends. My thanks to:
Connie, for her loving energy and encouragement, and our children,
Homer and Lyle, for their enthusiasm.
Barry Lippman, my editor at New American Library, for initiating this
project and his continued guidance and faith.
Larry Jones and Robert Golub for their skill and assistance in the
making of architecture.
G. W. Davison-Ackley for his commitment to an ecologically balanced
environment.

CONTENTS

ix

THE
ENERGY
EFFICIENT
HOME

INTRODUCTION

Your Energy Burden

Energy bills are not monthly dues you have to pay. Look at each one as a budgetary expense which you can control. You may be intimidated by the machinery which produces and consumes energy, but the more you discover how to control your energy usage, the more you will appreciate the services you receive.

You pay for energy according to the units consumed: electricity (kwh), gas (therms or cu. feet), or oil (gallons). Prepare an energy profile for your home by recording how many units of each energy source you have been using per month for the past year. If you don't have your past receipts, your utility company will supply copies. Analyze your energy bills to see how much you are paying for each service. Every home has a different pattern of consumption because of location, construction, equipment, and personal habits of the household, but energy-saving methods will definitely reduce the units you consume. This is your hedge against escalating energy prices. Energy conservation will not hold down the price per unit, but will help keep down your own energy bills. In addition, you will be reducing the deterioration of our environment and our growing dependence on foreign fuel supplies.

Every measure that eliminates energy waste—from turning off a light to installing a solar energy system—will help achieve these personal and national goals. Since most of us are buying a lot of extra energy to make up for the waste caused by standard home construction and inefficient personal habits, a thorough effort to build an energy-efficient household is far more effective than performing an occasional hit-or-miss task. You can adopt the energy conservation ethic at home without sacrificing your present levels of comfort and convenience.

Most houses use a combination of energy sources. These are the common household services and the forms of energy you can conserve:

Heating—gas, oil, or electricity
Cooling—electricity
Water Heating—gas, oil, or electricity

Appliances—electricity or gas
Lighting—electricity

Now look around your home carefully and consider the possibilities available to you:

☐ Using the sun, wind, and trees for heating, ventilation, and protection.
☐ Adding insulation to keep the heat inside in winter and keep the heat outside in hot weather.
☐ Reducing the amount of air leaking into the house through cracks and loose joints.
☐ Maintaining heating and cooling equipment for efficient operation.
☐ Reducing the use of hot water.
☐ Using fewer lights and more efficient lighting products.
☐ Operating appliances more efficiently.
☐ Reducing water usage, from leaky faucets to excessive waste disposal.
☐ Using solar energy systems to supplement existing heating and hot water equipment.
☐ Getting more fireplace heat into the room instead of up the chimney.
☐ Installing a wind generator to supplement the supply of electricity.

The purpose of this book is to help you take control over your energy burden. Part I will help you reduce the amount of energy you are using.

☐ With no expense of your time or money you will learn energy-saving habits.
☐ Low-cost improvements which you can do at home will quickly pay for themselves in energy savings.
☐ When you hire a contractor or serviceman you will know what to ask for and how to check his work. Proper installation and maintenance of equipment increases energy efficiency.

Part II of the book will introduce you to methods to supplement or replace your existing energy sources. It provides basic information about equipment, installation, maintenance, and costs for your home.

The depleting supply of gas and oil is driving up the prices. In Britain, four hundred years ago, the diminishing supply of wood caused a similar energy crisis which led to the development of coal as the primary energy source. This period of transition caused vast scientific and industrial changes. In today's shortage of fossil fuels, we are turning to alternative energy sources. We have the opportunity to develop *renewable* sources, such as solar and wind power. With modern forestation techniques we can also turn to wood power as a renewable resource.

Solar energy, wood, and wind power—as compared to electricity from a central power plant or fuel combustion in your home—are less costly to operate, non-polluting, and totally renewable.

The widespread transition from fossil fuels to renewable power sources is just beginning, and you can find out how to apply them in your own home. The basic technology is not mysterious, but it often requires a substantial financial investment.

NOTE: Throughout the text, products which, at the time of this writing, are still difficult for the consumer to locate are referred to by the manufacturer's name. Product performances described throughout the book are intended to help you select widely known products which best accommodate your energy saving needs, without recommending specific brands.

ENERGY CONSERVATION

PART 1

1

YOUR HOUSE LOCATION—
MAXIMIZING ENERGY ADVANTAGES

Climatic Regions

The continental United States can be divided into four general climatic regions. Each region is defined by general weather patterns which help to identify the priorities of home energy usage.

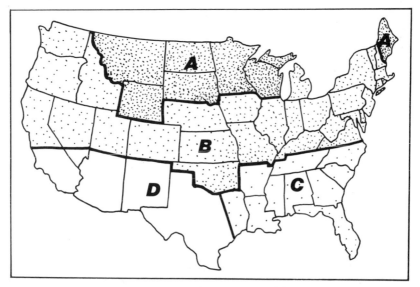

1. Climatic regions of the United States
A) Cool, B) Temperate, C) Hot-Humid, D) Hot-Arid

COOL REGION:	TEMPERATE REGION:	HOT-HUMID REGION:	HOT-ARID REGION:
cold winters	cool winters	hot days	hot days
mild summers	warm summers	warm nights	cool nights
winds from	high precipitation	high humidity	winds along the
the northwest	high humidity	variable winds	east-west axis
and southeast			low humidity
			clear skies

You can adapt your house to be more responsive to the climatic demands by maximizing your use of advantageous natural forces and minimizing the impact of the hostile elements. You can provide appropriate landscaping and simple architectural modifications around your house. These methods involve no mechanical power to improve or maintain your level of indoor comfort and are considered as *passive* environmental improvements.

While each of the four climatic regions has inherent variations and overlapping weather conditions, they do all exist within the Northern Hemisphere and share a constant southern exposure to the sun.

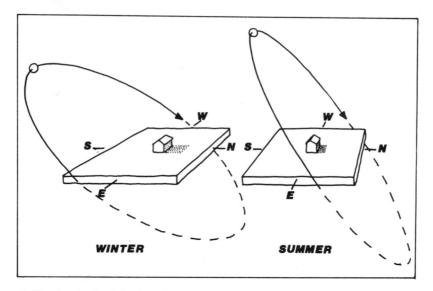

2. The low path of the sun during the winter can provide direct sunlight and warmth through south-facing windows. In the summer the sun rises north of east and sets north of west, causing twice as much solar-heat gain on the east and west as on the north and south walls.

Your house may not be laid out toward the climatically optimal orientation. But there are Early American homes, such as New England "salt boxes," which were built to take advantage of the sun's path and the local weather conditions. This energy-saving tradition can be traced to the earliest human dwelling and has been largely abandoned since the advent of mechanical heating and cooling systems powered by cheap fuel. But the time has come to adapt your home so that it can more effectively respond to your environment.

Maximizing Your Site— Sun and Wind Control

You already know your climatic region and whether you pay more for heating or cooling the house. Now find out the orientation—the sides of your house which most closely face the compass directions. Since each side is exposed to different weather conditions, you should adapt them accordingly. With new construction you can design a home with optimal considerations for site planning and orientation, but for your existing home the following measures will significantly reduce the energy burden. (For general sun and wind control devices recommended in each region, refer to Chart 1.)

———————————Chart 1———————————

Sun and Wind Control *

	Cool Region	Temperate Region	Hot-Humid Region	Hot-Arid Region
Horizontal Window/ Wall Overhang	S, SW, W, SE, E	S, SW, W, SE, E	S, SW, W, SE, E, NW, NE	S, SW, W, SE, E, NW, NE, N
Vertical Window/ Wall Baffle	W, E, NW, NE, N	W, E, NW, NE, N	W, E, NW, NE, N	W, E, NW, NE, N
Reflective Window Film			S, SW, W, SE, E	S, SW, W, SE, E
Evergreen Trees (Windbreak)	N, NW, W, NE, E	N, NW, W, NE		
Deciduous Trees Summer—Shade Winter—Solar Penetration	S, SW, SE	S, SW, SE, E		S, SW, W, SE, E
High Canopy Trees (Shade)			S, SW, W, SE, NW, NE	
Earth Berms	N, NW, NE	N, NW		

*Orientations listed in order of priority.

5

Cool Region

Since your major need is for heating, your goal is to capture and store as much of the sun's energy as possible and to protect the house from the coldest winter winds.

On a sunny, cold day allow the direct sunlight to enter the south and southwest windows. The southwest afternoon exposure provides the most winter solar heat gain because of the high afternoon temperatures and lower sun angle. Reflective exterior surfaces—like snow and light colored paving—will increase the useful heat gained from the sun. Be sure to close off the windows as they cease to receive direct sunlight (see page 36—Thermal Barriers.) By nightfall all the windows should be thermally protected to prevent excessive heat loss and allow the stored heat to reradiate into the rooms.

You should seal tightly all windows on the north, northwest, and northeast exposures. Use extra glazing, plastic covers, thermal barriers, and caulking to reduce the extreme heat loss due to cold winds and the absence of direct sunlight (see Chapter 3). In extremely cold climates all the windows around the house should be tightly sealed.

You can protect the house from the winter winds by planting evergreen trees around the north, northwest, and northeast sides. They are most effective windbreaks when planted in clusters of varying sizes at least 50 feet from the house. Pine trees are less effective since their boughs do not grow close to the ground. Your local agricultural center can recommend the best trees for your specific climate.

You should also consider exterior natural insulation for the north,

3. *Earth berms provide good insulation for the exterior of your home. Heavy polyethylene sheeting will protect the house siding from the moisture in the soil.*

northwest, and northeast sides. Pile the earth several feet up against the siding with a weatherproofing barrier between them to create a naturally insulating *earth berm*. Or plant small dense shrubbery along the edges of the house.

If you don't have enough space for the large windbreaks you should consider building a simple fence on the north, northwest, and northeast to help deflect the winter winds. These trees, bushes, and/or fences will add to summertime comfort by directing cooling breezes around the house.

Deciduous (hardwood) trees are ideal for the south, southeast, and southwest sides of your house. During the cold winter the sunlight will pass through the bare branches and reach the windows and walls. During the summer they will shade these exposures from the direct sun.

Temperate Region

Seasonal changes require both cooling and heating your home. During the heating season, your goal is to let the sun in and block the winds. During the cooling season you want to block off the direct sun and encourage the wind flow around and through the house.

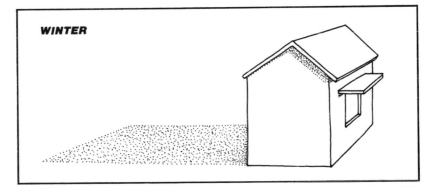

4, 5. On the south wall an overhang of the proper length will allow the winter sun to penetrate the window and effectively block off the direct sunlight during the summer.

During winter days, you should collect solar heat through the south and southwest windows, covering them at night and on overcast days. All the windows around the house should also be protected from heat loss throughout the season.

As the weather becomes warmer, you need to prevent the sun from striking and penetrating the windows and heating the rooms. Once the sunlight hits the window, you only partially keep the heat out with interior shades or blinds. On the south, southeast, southwest exposures you should build overhangs or install awnings to shade the glass surfaces. These may be either fixed in place, adjustable, or removable. Try to leave some air spaces between the overhang and the wall so that trapped hot air can escape. Keep in mind that a fixed overhang must not block the winter sun from reaching the glass.

Glass openings on the east and west cannot adequately be protected by a horizontal overhang because the sun is lower in the sky during the morning and afternoon. In addition to overhangs, vertical baffles attached to the wall on either side of the window will block most of the direct sunlight without eliminating your views.

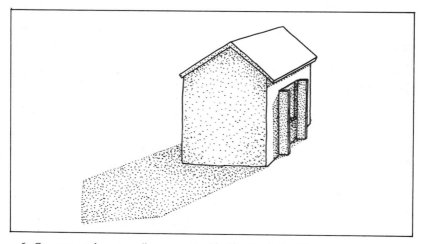

6. On east and west walls use vertical baffles to deflect the summer sun and the winter winds.

No shading protection is needed for the windows facing north and only a small amount on the northwest or northeast. You should ventilate the house with open windows, cross ventilation, and attic ventilation to offset the need for mechanical air conditioning.

Planting evergreens on the north and west exposures will create a winter windbreak as described under Cool Regions. The need for shading your house is more important in the temperate region. You should plant deciduous trees around the west, southwest, south, southeast, and eastern exposures. Depending on your exact location and heating-cooling ratio, you may use more evergreens (windbreaks) or deciduous trees (shading) on the east or west. The landscaping should encourage the summer breezes from the south and southwest to flow into the windows, through the rooms, and escape through open windows.

Hot-Humid Region

Your year-round comfort depends largely on making the house cool and dry. Protect the walls and windows from direct sunlight and provide as much ventilation as possible.

Install broad overhangs for the windows and walls on the south, and add vertical baffles to the east and west. Use jalousie windows with insect screening to allow the predominantly north-south breezes to ventilate the rooms. Increase cross ventilation with open windows in the upstairs rooms and attic ventilation. To reduce solar heat gain, apply *reflective films* to reflect direct sunlight. Close the window shades and blinds.

You want to maximize the air flow around the house near the ground level by planting *high-canopy* trees to shade the roof and walls throughout the year. Avoid low dense shrubs unless they direct the air flow to the house, or grow next to the walls providing a barrier to the sunlight.

Hot-Arid Region

Because of the generally clear days and low humidity, you experience hot days and cool nights. The wide daily temperature range is called the *diurnal swing.* You want to trap and isolate the daytime heat and release it into the rooms at night. During the winter, large south-facing glass areas can be used to collect daytime heat. At night, the glass surface must be closed to prevent heat loss. In the summer the windows on the north, east, and west should be protected from excessive heat gain with overhangs and opened whenever you can use the predominantly east-west breezes for ventilation.

If you are collecting heat on south-facing glass surfaces, plant deciduous trees on the southern exposure to allow winter sun penetration and summer shading. Vegetation along the east and west exposures will reduce the excessive solar heat gain.

Further Reading

1. Victor G. Olgyay, *Design with Climate,* Princeton, N. J.: Princeton University Press, 1963.

9

A moderately technical and comprehensive analysis of environmentally responsive building.

2. Bernard Rodofsky, *Architecture Without Architects,* New York: Museum of Modern Art, 1964.

A fascinating and beautifully illustrated analysis of environmentally balanced buildings utilizing natural forces.

YOUR BUILDING ENVELOPE—
CONTROLLING THE FLOW OF HEAT
THROUGH YOUR ROOFS, WALLS,
FLOORS, WINDOWS, BUILDING JOINTS,
AND DOORS

The roof, walls, and floors of a house form an envelope which maintains a comfortable indoor environment in spite of the weather. The previous chapter discusses methods of modifying your home and landscape to optimize the beneficial natural forces and minimize the effects of the hostile ones. This section will help you to better understand how the construction of roofs, walls, and floors can be improved as barriers against the extreme weather conditions.

Although most of our homes keep out rain and snow, they do not adequately retain heat in cold weather or block out heat in hot weather. We are forced to supply excessive amounts of heating or air conditioning. This excess, or wasted energy, may be as much as 30 percent of your energy costs. Proper construction and home repair methods greatly reduce this waste.

Thermal Insulation

Heat always flows from warm areas to colder ones. The intensity of this heat flow increases with the temperature difference between the areas. Each building material has an ability to retard the movement of heat through it, defined as the R (resistance) value. The higher the R value, the greater the resistance.

Uninsulated wood frame roofs, ceilings, walls, and floors have low R values such as R-3 to R-5. Adding insulation according to your climatic requirements and budget priorities will effectively reduce your heating and cooling bills.

In the days of cheap energy, low R-value construction was common. Now the added cost of high R-value construction is economically preferable because of increased energy costs.

A careful insulation investment in certain areas of your home will pay for itself within a few years with lowered heating and cooling bills. It will add to the resale value of your home by offering lower maintenance costs to the buyer. A program of home insulation should be combined with other energy conservation measures in order to maximize the dollar savings from your investment.

You can do many insulation installations by yourself in a day or two. Keep in mind that each climatic region requires different solutions and that each home presents unique conditions.

Before insulating you must look for the material which best fits your project. Insulation is sold in several shapes and is composed of different materials. First, select the *shape* you need to properly fill the area to be insulated. Then choose the *material* with the best qualities for your needs.

Shapes

Batts are precut sections either 15 or 23 inches wide designed to fit between wood joists or rafters in standard frame construction. They range from 1 to 7 inches thick to fit within the space between the interior and exterior finish materials in standard frame construction. For easy handling, they come in 4 and 8-foot lengths. You can usually buy them with vapor barriers applied to one surface. For existing homes, batts are handy for unfinished attic floors, ceilings, and the underside of floors. Batts are made of glass fiber or rock wool.

Rolls or *Blankets* are essentially the same as batts except the lengths are not precut. They are more difficult to handle but can be used with less waste if carefully fitted.

Loose-Fill, Poured, is small, tufted bits of material made from glass fiber, rock wool, cellulosic fiber, vermiculite, or perlite. It is sold in bags and is easy to install on existing unfinished attic floors; pour by hand and level with a garden rake. A vapor barrier (usually plastic sheeting) is installed separately.

Loose-Fill, Blown In is similar in form to loose-fill, poured, except that this variety is blown in by a contractor using pneumatic equipment. It is used to insulate areas inaccessible for batts or rolls—such as walls, floors, and ceilings with finished interior surfaces—and where the structural framing is irregular or where there are obstructions in the space to be insulated. Made from glass fiber, rock wool, or cellulosic fiber.

Rigid Boards are panels either 2 or 4 feet wide by 8 feet long, available from ¾ to 4 inches thick. Used in existing homes for basement wall insulation. Made of polystyrene or urethane.

Foam-in-Place is a relatively new technique for use in wood-frame construction. Initial high insulation values are qualified by untested long-term benefits, high costs, and potential hazards. Materials being used are ureaformaldehyde (UF) foam and polyurethane foam, pumped into cavity spaces between joists.

Materials

Glass Fiber and *Rock Wool* are both made from mineral substances such as glass, rock, or slag which is processed from a molten state into the fibrous form. They are inexpensive materials, moisture-resistant and fire-resistant. When used as loose-fill, either poured or blown in, they have two disadvantages: an inability to reach through tight obstructions and a tendency to settle after a time. So it is difficult to guarantee complete coverage. These fibers can irritate your skin during application. Also rock wool is especially susceptible to damage from moisture.

Cellulosic Fiber is made from wastepaper products such as newspapers. It is shredded and milled into a low-density fluffy material and sold in bags for poured and blown-in applications. It is second only to glass fiber as the most widely used insulating material. It has a smaller tuft size and fills more thoroughly than glass fiber or rock wool. It must be chemically treated to provide fire retardancy. When treated with boric acid (*boron-based cellulose*) it is both fire-retardant and fungus-resistant. But many manufacturers have been substituting aluminum sulfate or ammonium sulfate for the boric acid. Recent analysis has shown that these chemicals absorb excessive moisture and support fungal growth which deteriorate the insulation value of the material. Be sure to look for products treated only with *boric acid.*

Vermiculite and *Perlite* are mineral products used as loose-fill materials. Although expensive, they can be used economically to fill in small, tight areas you can't get to with other fill materials. Used especially in finished walls with many pipes and wires, they have a tendency to absorb moisture and settle, leaving gaps above.

Polystyrene and *Rigid Polyurethane* are made of plastic. They have very high R values and are moisture-resistant, but are not fire-resistant. If they are used to insulate an existing interior basement wall, you must cover them with a fire-protective material such as ½-inch gypsum wallboard. In new construction, they are used for exterior sheathing and concrete slab and foundation insulation.

Urethane Foam Spray is not recommended for residential installations because when it burns it releases toxic fumes. Despite its high insulating value, the fire and fume hazard coupled with the material, installation, and protection costs make it unsuitable for home use.

Ureaformaldehyde (UF) Foam is sprayed between the joists by trained installers. It has been used for years in Northern Europe as insulation for masonry cavity walls, but it is the most controversial of the new techniques. Standards and specifications for UF foam use in the United States are currently being developed by the National Bureau of Standards. Extensive testing has caused the Canadian government to lower the manufacturers' claimed R value by 60 percent and the Canadian Central Mortgage and Housing Corporation has banned its use. The major problem with UF foam results from the water which is present in the foam during application. Over a period of time, water causes shrinkage, deterioration of adjacent building materials, reduced thermal resistance, and often excessive odor of formaldehyde. NBS testing suggests that it should not be applied in areas subject to high temperatures and high humidity, such as attics and ceilings. It is not recommended for any insulation use until industry standards are established for material specifications and installation procedure.

———————————————Chart 2———————————————

Insulation Material	R Value per Inch Thickness
Batts or Blankets	
Glass Fiber	3.1
Rock Wool	3.1
Loose-Fill, Poured	
Glass Fiber	2.3
Rock Wool	3.1
Cellulosic Fiber	3.7
Vermiculite	2.1
Perlite	2.6
Foam-in-Place	
Ureaformaldehyde foam	4.8
Polyurethane foam	6.0
Rigid Boards	
Polystyrene	4.5
Urethane	5.9

Vapor Barriers

During cold weather, the normal indoor household activity can release at least three gallons of water vapor each day. Some of the moisture does escape through the openings around doors, windows, and by mechanical ventilation. But a lot of moisture migrates to the outside through the roof and walls. The water vapor moves into the construction until it touches a cold surface, where it condenses and may form as water, ice, or frost inside the wall or roof. You can see the condensate on your windows. When it occurs in roofs and walls it can warp and stain exterior wood siding and cause peeling of the paint as well as destroy the insulation.

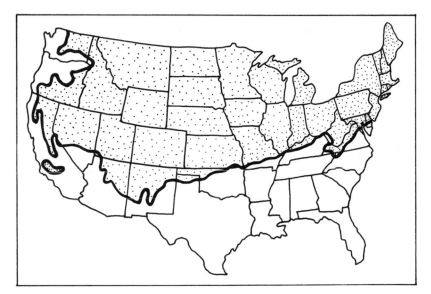

7. Homes located in the shaded portion of the map will benefit most from vapor-barrier protection.

The amount of moisture vapor a material permits through its surface is called its *perm (permeability) value.* You should ask about the material's perm value just as you should ask about the R value of insulation. For ceilings, walls, and floors a value of .25 perms is recommended.

Materials

Integral Vapor Barriers are thin membranes attached to the face of

15

insulation batts, blankets, or conventional gypsum wallboards. The surface is usually a kraft paper or aluminum foil. The vapor barrier should face the warm side of the house unless your climate is very humid. Protect the vapor-barrier surface with fire-resistant finishing materials.

---------- Chart 3 ----------

Pints of Water

Plants	1.7 for each plant in 24 hours
Showers	.5 for each shower
Baths	.1 for each bath
Floor Mopping	2.9 per 100 square feet
Kettles and Cooking	5.5 per day
Clothes (Washing, Steam Ironing, Drying)	29.4 per week

Plastic Sheeting makes an excellent vapor barrier. You can buy it in large rolls wherever you get insulation materials. For unfinished surfaces, staple a layer of 4- or 6-mil polyethylene film on the warm side of the insulation. Protect the vapor barrier with fire-resistant finish material, such as fire-code gypsum wallboard.

Vapor Impermeable Paints and Papers When you are blowing in insulation through small holes in existing walls, floors, or ceilings, there is no feasible way to develop a vapor barrier inside the frame construction. The best method to keep interior moisture from moving through and condensing on the insulation or adjacent surface is to treat the interior finished surface. A first coat of oil-based enamel paint covered with an alkyd-base second coat provides an excellent vapor barrier. If you can add a layer or two of aluminum-spray enamel it will increase the surface resistance to moisture penetration. Vinyl wall coverings will also help. For existing floors, try penetrating floor sealants, varnish, or wax coats as vapor barriers. Everything you can do to keep the interior moisture from deteriorating your insulation will help reduce your energy bills.

Ventilation

Crawl spaces and attics should be ventilated. Attic ventilation will help prevent moisture condensation during cold weather and expel the trapped hot air in warm weather. In crawl spaces ventilation is needed to reduce the condensation only in cold climates. The proper ventilation depends on the size and shape of the attic or crawl space.

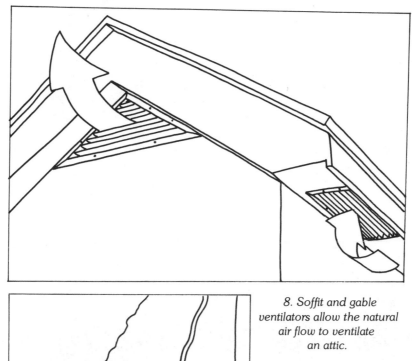

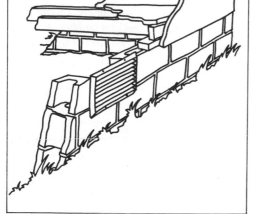

8. Soffit and gable ventilators allow the natural air flow to ventilate an attic.

9. To ventilate a crawl space, replace one of the concrete blocks with a foundation ventilator.

Ventilation through insulated ceilings, walls, and floors will allow small amounts of air to circulate through the insulation to dry out any accumulated moisture. This is especially important where you have no vapor barrier to block the moisture penetration.

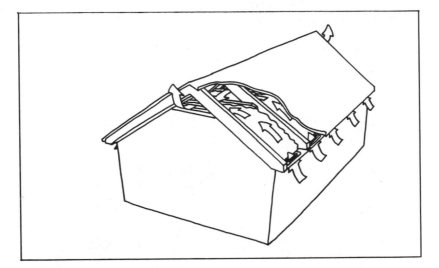

10. *When insulating a finished attic, be sure to provide ventilation between the insulation and the roof surface.*

Home Insulation Projects

Before 1945 most American homes were built without any insulation at all. If your house was built since then there is likely to be some insulation—but probably not enough. The following map shows recommended insulation R values for roofs, walls, and floors throughout the country.

You should make the following analysis before spending any money.

1. Decide which areas to insulate.
2. Find out how much insulation you already have.
3. Compare your existing R value to the recommended values in your area.
4. Choose the best materials for your job.
5. Decide to do it yourself or hire a contractor.

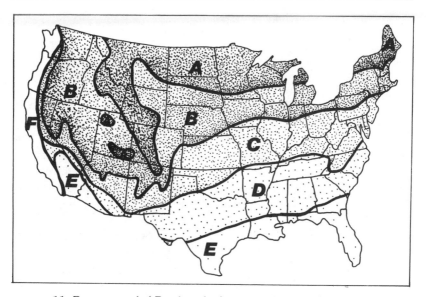

11. *Recommended R values for home insulation (adapted from Owen-Corning):*

A)	Ceiling 38	Wall 19	Floor 22
B)	Ceiling 33	Wall 19	Floor 22
C)	Ceiling 30	Wall 19	Floor 19
D)	Ceiling 26	Wall 19	Floor 13
E)	Ceiling 26	Wall 13	Floor 11
F)	Ceiling 19	Wall 11	Floor 11

Do-It-Yourself. You can probably do several of these projects yourself in about one day and save the contractor's fee—usually 50 percent of the total cost. This kind of work requires very little skill but a lot of caution. Here are some safety tips to reduce the chance of accidents:

1. The materials are itchy and the locations cramped so wear gloves, inexpensive breathing masks, and a hard hat.
2. Don't smoke during the job.
3. Keep the insulation in the wrappers until you begin.
4. Provide temporary lighting.
5. Provide the following tools: tape measure, heavy-duty staple gun or hammer and tacks, heavy-duty shears or matt knife, and duct tape.
6. When you are done, wash the work clothes separately.

Hiring a Contractor. If you decide not to do the work yourself, it is always worth the effort to search for the right contractor to work in your home. The work may disrupt your life to some extent, but being confident of the contractor's responsibilities and reliability will minimize the inevitable anxiety.

1. Locate three or four contractors: Yellow Pages under Insulation Contractors; friends or neighbors; local government Energy Conservation office; Home Builders Association.

2. Check reliability: call local Better Business Bureau; call customer references.

3. Get estimates: written list of services and materials; areas to be insulated; materials to be used (R values); methods to be used; cleanup and patching if required; time estimated to complete the work; Contractors' Certificates of Insurance; total contract cost. Cost overruns within the contract are the contractor's responsibility. Extra work beyond the contract should be negotiated separately.

4. Contractor selection: Don't choose a contractor on the basis of price alone. A contractor may give a low estimate if he is not busy at the time. Remember that a contractor's reliability is the true measure of his value.

Attics

The top of your house is by far the *first priority* for insulation: In cold weather it will prevent the most extreme loss of heat and in hot weather it will keep heat out.

Your attic may be an unfinished space with exposed floor joists. This is the easiest area to insulate yourself. Be careful not to step in the space between the joists or you will probably break through the ceiling of the room below.

If there is no insulation:

☐ Buy the batts or blankets with vapor-barrier backing and place them with the vapor barrier side down. You may need two layers of batt or blanket insulation. Lay the first layer between the joists and the second layer running the opposite direction on top of the joists.

☐ If the batts or blankets have no vapor-barrier backing or you use loose-fill, place a polyethylene sheet vapor barrier before installing the insulation.

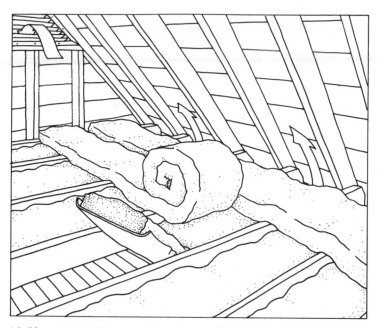

12. You may need to install two layers of blanket insulation to achieve the adequate R value. Note the vapor barrier is on the bottom of the first layer only.

13. When installing loose-fill insulation, pour it over a securely stapled polyethylene vapor barrier.

If there is already insulation there, it is probably lying on the floor space between the wood joists. Measure the insulation thickness.

1. Use Chart 2 to find the R value of the insulation you have. If it is inadequate, measure the length and width of the space to find the square feet of insulation you will need.
2. See Illustration 11 for the recommended R values in your area.
3. Don't use a vapor barrier between the old and the new. Just place the batts, blankets, or loose-fill over the existing insulation between the joists.
4. Paint or paper the ceiling below; use vapor impermeable materials.

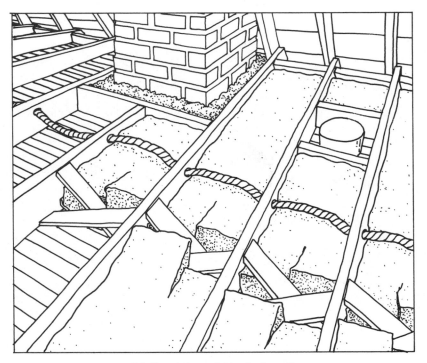

14. Special conditions in the attic:
1. Use loose-fill with no vapor barrier near the chimney.
2. Don't insulate within 3 inches of a recessed light fixture.
3. Don't stuff batts into the wood bridges. Insulation loses R value when compressed.

When your attic has a finished floor, the walls and ceiling may be unfinished. Before insulating, decide whether or not you want to make the space into a usable room.

Unoccupied attic with finished floor. If you choose to close off the attic space, you need only insulate the attic floor. You can rent equipment to blow loose insulation into the attic floor or hire a contractor for the job. This will stop your valuable heat from migrating up into the unoccupied space. Provide ventilation to eliminate summer heat buildup. Remove some floorboards and blow the insulation into the space between the attic floor and the ceiling of the rooms below.

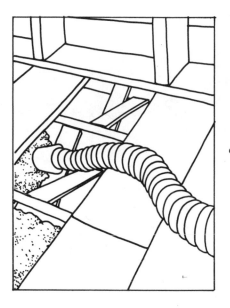

15. Remove floorboards at crossbridging to blow insulation into an attic floor.

Occupied attic with finished floor. If you want to make the attic livable, do not insulate the attic floor. Insulating only the walls and roof allows the heat to rise into the room and keeps the space cooler in the summer. If the walls and ceiling are covered with an interior finish material (wood paneling, drywall, or plaster) you should blow in insulation. Fill the spaces between the interior finish material and the exterior finish material (siding or shingles). Many attics have small walls and ceilings built inside the actual roof. Be sure that the insulation fills all the surfaces necessary to enclose both the finished attic room and the rest of the house below.

When you want to use the attic as a room and the walls and ceiling are unfinished, use batts or blankets in between the studs and rafters, then finish these surfaces.

Be sure to provide adequate ventilation.

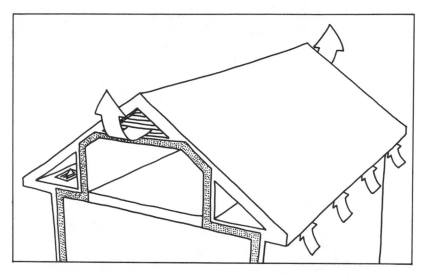

16. Note areas to insulate around a livable attic space.

NOTE: When your attic is properly insulated, the next priority for cost-effective weatherproofing is to seal the air leaks around the house. Caulking and weatherstripping are inexpensive and easy to apply. If your budget permits, consider insulating the exterior walls, exposed floors, and basement walls.

Exterior Walls

To find out if the wall is insulated, remove the cover of a light switch or electric outlet and inspect the wall cavity. If you already have some insulation it does not pay to add more. But *do* consider protecting it with a vapor barrier. First, seal all interior cracks, especially around door and window frames. Then a good vapor impermeable paint or vinyl wall covering will help reduce moisture penetration.

NOTE: If there is no insulation, don't spend money here until all the doors and windows have been weatherproofed. Then, if your budget permits, insulate the walls.

In some older wood-frame homes, the wall cavity is clear all the way up to the attic. Make sure the cavity is closed at the foundation and then you can pour loose-fill from the attic into the spaces between the studs.

In conventional 2 x 4-inch wood stud frame walls the attic opening is blocked and you will need to blow in insulation. This is a project you can do yourself with rented equipment. Here is a step-by-step explanation of the task:

1. Drill holes from the outside, unless you have a brick facing over the stud walls.
2. You must fill each space between the studs, which are usually 15 inches apart.
3. Drill the holes just below any horizontal wood framing—either blocking or fire stops—and blow down to fill up the cavity.
4. Fill the space above and below windows and above the doors.
5. Two-story houses are more difficult. You have to drill another set of holes and blow in from the top of the second story wall.

Exposed Floors

There may be a floor without a heated space below it. Some examples are: 1) floor raised above the ground on columns; 2) floor extending beyond the lower walls; 3) above an unheated garage. It is usually easier to insulate the crawl space walls than the floors above the crawl space. If you can conveniently insulate the floors, that is preferable.

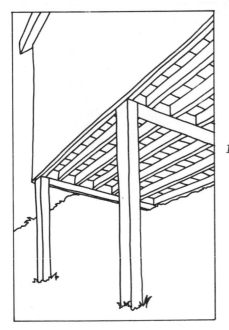

17. A home on a sloping site often has exposed floors which require insulation.

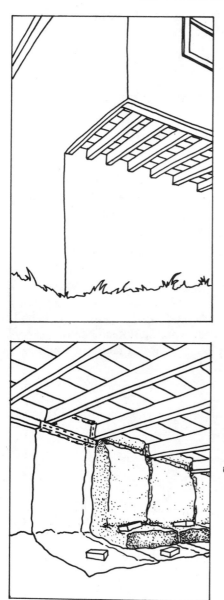

18. *A floor which extends beyond any lower walls requires insulation.*

19. *Secure the vapor barrier and insulation to a crawl space wall with nailing strips along the wood header. Use bricks as weights on the ground.*

It is a relatively inexpensive job to insulate the floor and reduce heat loss considerably.

- ☐ Refer to Illustration 11 for the recommended R value.
- ☐ Use batts with integral vapor barriers and place the barrier side up toward the inside of the house.
- ☐ If you use foil-faced batts, keep the facing ¾ of an inch below the flooring to radiate heat back into the house.
- ☐ If you use kraft paper-faced batts, fit them tight up against the flooring.
- ☐ To hold the batts in place attach chicken wire, wire mesh, or wood strips to the bottom of the joists.
- ☐ While you are there, use the same insulation to wrap all exposed air ducts and plumbing pipes.

Basement Walls

In a heated basement you are losing heat through the walls unless they are insulated. The problem is most severe above the outside ground level to several feet below it. As the walls get deeper into the ground, the earth acts as a natural insulator. In climates where there is a shallow frost you should insulate the basement walls from the ceiling to 2 feet below the ground line. In colder climates, insulate the full height of the wall.

The basement walls are usually concrete masonry construction. If there are wood studs and a finished material in the space you can follow the procedures for blowing in loose-fill insulation.

If the concrete walls are exposed, the least difficult method is to attach furring strips to the wall with *masonry nails* and apply rigid insulating

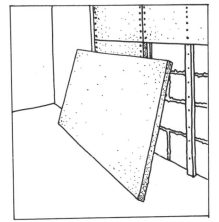

20. Add rigid board insulation to the walls of a basement. Note the finished wall covering placed over the boards for fire resistance.

boards over them. Then you will have to cover the boards with a fire-resistant finish material.

Another method is to attach a full stud wall to the concrete wall and fill it with batts facing the vapor barrier into the room, then apply the finish material. Both jobs require several days of carpentry to achieve adequate insulation and a good finished appearance.

The insulation of *crawl space floors, concrete slabs,* and *foundations* is generally too difficult and costly on existing homes.

Caulking

Many homes in cold, windy climates lose as much as 50 percent of their heat through leaks around windows, doors, and construction joints. You should seal these leaks with caulking material which is easily and inexpensively applied from a tube in a caulking gun. Sealing the leaks will also prevent water seepage into the construction which may rot the materials and deteriorate the insulation.

To locate the air leaks, pass a lighted candle over the following surfaces:

☐ where the window frame meets the wall.
☐ where the door frame meets the wall.
☐ where the door frame meets the exterior siding.

You need to apply the caulk wherever the flame waves. First, clean out the cracks with a screwdriver or narrow wire brush. Then fill them with a strip of sponge rubber or fiberglass insulation before caulking. An excellent filler for large gaps is *oakum,* a specially treated hemp rope available in plumbing supply stores.

Urethane caulk is sold in cartridges that fit into ordinary caulking guns. It is easy to apply, will adhere to any building material, and can be painted. It will stretch to keep the gap covered during the normal movement of the building materials due to weather changes. It should last up to twenty years.

Hypalon and *Silicones* are similar to the urethane but you must prime coat any porous material (wood, masonry) to which the caulk will be applied.

Latex, Butyl, and *Polyvinyl* caulks are less expensive but not as durable. Some products shrink or crack after a few years.

Oil- or *Resin-* based caulks are the least expensive. They tend to dry out and crack, often losing effectiveness within a year or two, necessitating another caulking job.

Lead base caulk is not recommended. Many states prohibit its use because it is considered toxic.

NOTE: There are several other parts of your house where two different materials come together, possibly creating an air leak and require caulking:

21. Check these areas for air leaks which should be caulked.

Exterior surfaces: at the corners where the siding meets the trim; at the base where the siding meets the foundation; where the siding meets the masonry chimney; where electric outlets and water lines pass through an exterior wall; door frames.

Inside the house: where pipes, wires, or light fixtures penetrate the ceiling of an unheated attic; where the furnace flue goes through a flat roof or ceiling of an unheated attic, or an unheated basement or crawl space.

Weatherstripping

Windows

If the window sash fits loosely in the frame, air is leaking through and in many cases accounts for 30 percent of the heat loss in your house. Adding weatherstripping is easy, inexpensive, and will rapidly pay for itself in energy savings.

Weatherstripping materials are applied to the edges of the window sash or on the frames to close the gaps between them. The type of weatherstripping to use depends on the kind of windows you have. All of the materials are available from hardware stores or home supply centers. Inexpensive nailed-on felt strips should be used only as *temporary* weatherstripping. More durable types are better investments—they are

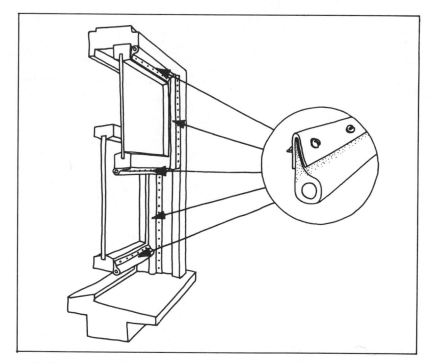

22. Cut vinyl weatherstripping to fit each part of the window sash or frame. The strip along the side of the lower frame will usually make it impossible to open the upper sash.

more effective and longer lasting. You should also select the weatherstripping material best suited for each type of window:

Double-hung and sliding windows. The first choice for durability and easy installation is *rolled vinyl.* It is nailed in place around the window and is visible after installation. It is available with a metal backing to provide more secure attachment and less friction when the windows are moving. A good alternate is a *thin spring metal.* It is harder to install but once in place cannot be seen. It is sold in rolls and is either nailed into place or applied with a self-sticking adhesive backing.

Casement and awning windows. These are easier to weatherstrip because they move from a hinged edge and have fewer problems of friction. The easiest solution is a *vinyl gasket* which you can buy in rolls and cut to slip over the lip of the window frame. A less expensive alternative is adhesive-backed foam in strips. They are applied to the frame to seal the gap when the window closes.

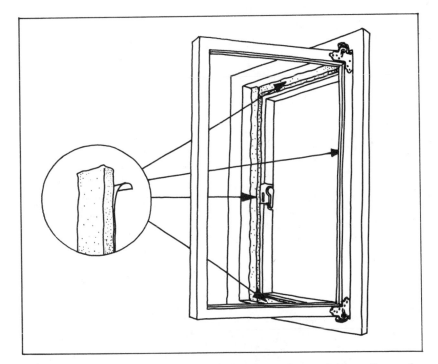

23. Adhesive-backed foam strips will compress to form a tight weather seal when a casement or awning window is closed.

Jalousie windows. You can weatherstrip each pane of glass by slipping a clear vinyl channel over the edges. Since these windows are made with overlapping but unsealed louvers, the weatherstripping also reduces the air conditioning load in summer.

Doors

The problem of air infiltration around the frame is more important than the flow of heat through the door itself. *Storm doors* are less cost-effective than storm windows unless your entry door has glass panels.

You should carefully check the air leaks between the door and the frame. The gaps are likely to be bigger than those around your windows. Your door may not hang properly, so check the hinges. Tightening the hinges can help align the door to the frame and reduce the gaps. In cold climates you should plan to weatherstrip the door. If there is a glass panel in the door, check it for leaks and caulk it if necessary.

The top and both sides of the door can be easily weatherstripped at little cost. You can apply adhesive-backed foam all around the inside edge of the door frame.

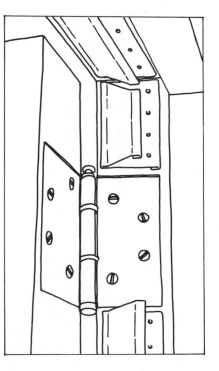

24. Use spring metal strips on an exterior door. Cut the spring metal strips to avoid the door hinges. Face the grooved opening to the inside of the house.

More durable materials such as spring metal cost more and must be tacked into place. The installation is similar to window weatherstripping but generally easier.

If you are a good handyman use interlocking metal channels or J-strips. These installations require aligned metal strips on the door and the frame which mate when the door is closed, forming an excellent seal. The materials and workmanship, however, must be precise.

The bottom of the door must be treated differently. The door swings over the threshold—a raised wood or metal strip which divides the interior flooring from the outside surface. To seal this gap you can either attach a *door sweep* to the door or install a new threshold with a flexible vinyl insert.

If your threshold is level across its length, the door sweep is the easier task. It is sold as a rubber seal in a metal channel mount, which you cut to size and screw to the inside of the door. The rubber seal will wear out after a while but is easily replaced.

In older homes the thresholds may be unevenly worn away or even cracked and porous. Replacing the threshold with a tight sealing unit is

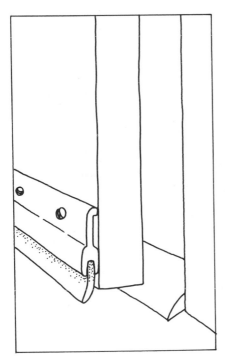

25. Door sweep attached to the inside of an entry door prevents air leakage through the bottom of the door.

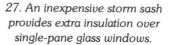

*27. An inexpensive storm sash
provides extra insulation over
single-pane glass windows.*

recommended. You can buy these in hardware stores or home supply centers. The installation requires some minor carpentry in taking out the existing threshold and fitting the new one. As with the door top and side weatherstripping, there are more sophisticated interlocking seals which are difficult for the homeowner to install, but the object is to close the gap as economically as possible. In this case the cost of installing and occasionally replacing the rubber seal is as effective and less expensive than the interlocking metal weatherstripping.

Storm Windows

If you have single-pane windows which need caulking and weatherstripping, you should consider investing in storm windows. You can buy or build a fixed *storm sash* to place outside your existing window. It can be either a clear acrylic sheet ¼-inch thick or plate glass in a wooden frame. (It will transfer 10 percent less heat than a metal frame.) Make sure it fits tightly over the exterior window frame. Small-drilled holes in the bottom sash will permit water from condensation to escape. These can be built or bought and installed for about ten to fifteen dollars per window, and will effectively cut heat loss through the window by about 45 percent. The only drawback is that you will not be able to open the window. They can be taken down in mild weather.

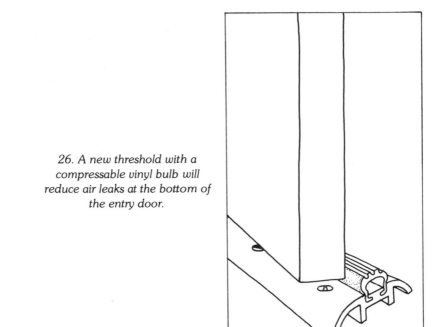

26. A new threshold with a compressable vinyl bulb will reduce air leaks at the bottom of the entry door.

Replacement windows are a more expensive solution. Prefabricated units fit over your existing windows or completely replace them. These are the double or triple-track *combination storm windows* so widely advertised. Double or triple glazing and screens are available. The triple-glazed units are recommended only in extremely cold climates. While the double glass reduces heat loss by about 50 percent over single panes, the third pane reduces heat loss by an additional 15 percent. Again, the wood frames are preferred.

Some units are being made with vinyl or aluminum shields over the wood frames. Be sure, if you buy these or all-metal frames, that they have plastic thermal breaks built in. They should also be fully weatherstripped and have holes for condensation escape. You can order these units and then install them yourself—reducing the cost to about thirty-five dollars per window.

Thermal Barriers

For windows which are well sealed against leaks, you can control the heat loss through the glass with home-built movable thermal barriers.

☐ On a cold night or cloudy day you want to reduce the heat loss; on a sunny winter day you want to let the sun's heat into the house—through south-facing glass.

☐ On a hot summer day you want to keep out the heat.

☐ On a cool summer night you may want to let the interior heat pass through the glass. Or if your house is air-conditioned you want to keep the cool air inside.

The point is that, unlike roof, wall, or floor insulation, window insulation should be movable.

The normal devices used to cover a window, such as shades and blinds, regulate the light but have no real value in controlling heat loss. They will help somewhat during warm weather to block the sun and reduce the air-conditioning burden. Curtains which reach to the floor can be counterproductive by blocking the heating elements, preventing the flow of heat into the room, and sending it right out the window. But you should look for insulating fabrics to attach onto the window side of your shades or drapes. You can also buy one-inch thick polystyrene boards, cut them to fit inside the window frame, and temporarily attach them with hook-and-eye catches or magnetic clips.

Insulated Shutters

The easy do-it-yourself solution is to cover the glass area with tight-fitting insulated shutters or shades. They can cut heat loss through a single glazed window by as much as 70 percent.

These shutters are installed on the inside of the window and can be arranged to slide over the window in a track or fold over the window on hinges. They can be made to fit each window in your house. The cost for the material is low, but it will take some time to measure, cut, and install the shutters. Be sure to check with your fire department that the insulating material does not create a fire hazard.

Rigid insulation boards of polystyrene come in thicknesses of ½ to 2 inches. You can easily cut them at home to fit your windows. They are very lightweight, have excellent R values, and will work well either as sliding panels or hinged shutters. You can cover them with decorative fabric or wallpaper to make them design elements rather than obstrusive objects.

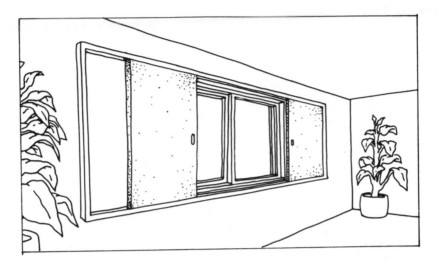

28, 29. Insulate windows with:
1. Thermal barriers sliding in a wooden track.
2. Hinged insulating shutters.

Plastic Covers

A simple, inexpensive, temporary thermal barrier is a thin layer of polyethylene tacked and taped onto the frame around your window. It will distort visibility through the window and look makeshift. But light will come through and it will significantly lower the heat loss through the glass. Clear, acrylic-plastic panels screwed onto the window frame will be more expensive, but will provide better thermal resistance and better appearance.

Further Reading

In the Bank . . . or up the Chimney?

Available from the U. S. Department of Housing and Urban Development. A booklet describing do-it-yourself home improvements with costing techniques.

HEATING, COOLING, AND LIGHTING EQUIPMENT

Space Heating

Many homeowners are unfamiliar with the mechanics of their heating systems. But whether you have a forced warm-air system or a hot-water system, there are some simple tasks you can do at home to reduce your fuel bills by improving the efficiency of the equipment. With electric resistance systems, however, there are fewer opportunities for the homeowner. Refer to Chart 3 which indicates the relationships of the components in each system. It is essential to have a reliable serviceman check and adjust your system before each heating season. With some knowledge of your equipment, you can be sure that many energy-saving opportunities are explored.

If you have a *forced warm-air system,* gas, oil, or electricity heats the air inside the furnace. A fan circulates the heated air through ducts into the rooms, and returns the cooler air from the rooms to the furnace. Dampers inside the ducts regulate the amount of circulating air and the thermostat controls the burner or circulating fan in accordance with the demand for heat in the house.

In a *hot-water heating system,* gas, oil, or electricity heats the water inside the boiler. A pump circulates the heated water through pipes to the room radiators, and returns the cooled water to the boiler. Valves regulate the flow through each piping circuit, and a thermostat controls the burner or circulating pump in accordance with the demand for heat in the house.

If your house is heated by *electric resistance,* the electricity is generated at power stations, controlled by utility companies, where it is produced by burning oil, gas, or coal, or with hydropower or nuclear power. This electricity is delivered directly to the consumer—no combustion or pollution at home—but at escalating prices in many regions. Inside the house, the meter spins as the electricity passes through wires to heat the resistance coils in your furnace, boiler, or baseboard units. If you use electricity to power a *heat pump* it is more efficient, saving between two and three times the electricity required for electric-resistance heating.

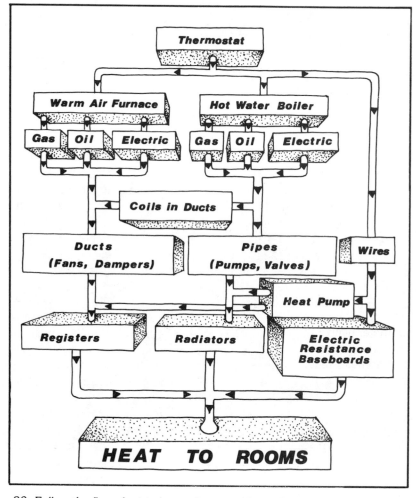

30. Follow the flow chart to locate the parts of your heating system activated when you turn on your thermostat.

Thermostats

From Illustration 30 you can see that the thermostat controls the whole works, and you control the thermostat. You set the thermostat at the desired temperature and this little device sends appropriate electric signals to the heating system to maintain the desired temperature. There may be just one thermostat for the whole house, or one for each area of a zoned heating system.

Location

A thermostat senses only the air temperature surrounding it to control the heating system. It should be located away from specific cool or warm places such as exterior walls or radiators. If you have one thermostat for the whole house, it should be located where it will monitor the average indoor temperature.

Calibration

Your thermostat may not be registering the temperature properly. If you set it at 72°F (22°C), it may be keeping the heat on when it is already 74°F (23°C) inside. To check the thermostat's accuracy, tape a thermometer (with a small pad behind it) to the wall next to the thermostat. If after 15 minutes there is a variation between the thermostat and the thermometer reading, try cleaning the inside of the thermostat. Take off the cover plate and remove any dust and clean the contact points gently. When the thermostat is off by two or three degrees, it can affect your fuel bill by as much as 6 to 9 percent. If you cannot correct the accuracy you can compensate by adjusting the setting according to the thermometer. You should replace a continuously fault thermostat with a new *timer control* model.

Setting

During the heating season, set your house thermostat to the lowest comfortable temperature. If there are several thermostats to control the zoned heating system, remember to adjust each one, heating some areas less than others, depending on your needs. Daytime settings between 65°F (18°C) and 65°F (20°C) provide adequate comfort except for elderly people. At night, turn the setting down to 60°F (15°C), sleep comfortably, and save 10 to 15 percent on your fuel bills. Nighttime thermostat "setbacks" can be controlled automatically.

41

Timer Control Thermostats

You can buy automatic timer units to add to your existing thermostat or as a complete replacement. Some models are sold with do-it-yourself installation instructions.

Clock thermostats will start and stop the setback period automatically. If you keep a regular schedule these are convenient controls.

Interval thermostats must be started manually like an oven timer. The setback period ends automatically at the end of the timer's cycle. These are less expensive than the clock thermostats.

Switch thermostats must be manually operated to start and stop the setback period and are not recommended since you can turn the temperature setting on your thermostat instead of using the switch which costs twenty dollars. More expensive switch models control several thermostats from a central location.

Photocell thermostats automatically start and stop the setback period when the surrounding light level changes. They are not recommended because you have to make sure the lighting or daylight is in the right place at the right time all year round. It's easier just to remember to change the thermostat setting.

If you do invest in a clock or interval timer thermostat it will cost about fifty dollars. Your fuel savings in the first few years will probably pay for this expenditure. Dependable thermostats are available at electric supply, hardware, and department stores. Look for the models you can install by yourself. If you are replacing the unit, be sure that the new thermostat is compatible with the wiring to your present thermostat. Some are two-wire units, similar to conventional thermostats, while others require three or more wires. Also be sure that the voltage requirements match your existing circuit.

Habits

When you are going to be away for a few days or more, lower the thermostat setting to 50°F (10°C) to protect the water systems from freezing. You can override any of the automatic setback thermostats by moving the dial.

When you come into the cold house, don't set the thermostat higher than the temperature you want; the heat will not come up any faster.

Keep in mind that significant heat is generated in your home by cooking, bright lighting, and groups of people. Take every opportunity to recognize this internal heat gain and turn down the thermostat accordingly.

In cold weather you may feel chilly if there is an uninsulated window in the room. Instead of turning up the thermostat, insulate the window.

Gas Furnaces

The money you spend to have a reliable serviceman tune-up and repair your furnace each fall can result in more energy savings than the service charge. If you follow your owner's manual to clean or change the

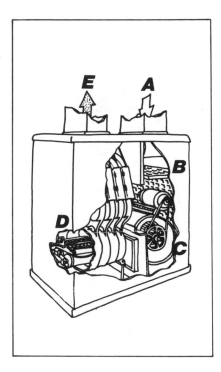

31. In a gas furnace the return air enters at (A), is circulated through filters (B) by blower (C). It is heated by burners (D) and supplied to the house through ducts (E).

filters, the serviceman can be directed to perform more technical tasks to improve the efficiency of the furnace. Ask him to check and adjust the following:

☐ Clean the opening (orifice) of the pilot light.
☐ Adjust the opening to bathe the thermocouple tube for proper ignition.
☐ Check the temperature at the start-up. If it's too hot, then heat is not being delivered soon enough and the blower must be adjusted.

☐ Check the belts on the blower for slipping.
☐ Exhaust gas analysis and temperature.
☐ Drafts.
☐ Flame pattern.
☐ Air stat setting.
☐ Possible reduction of the orifice size to increase fuel efficiency.

Oil Burners

You can perform a few maintenance tasks on the oil burner. The oil burner sprays a fine mist of oil into the combustion chamber of the furnace or boiler where an electric spark ignites it. Using the owner's manual, make the following adjustments:

☐ Lubricate the fan motor.
☐ Clean the air blower, the exhaust stack, and the stack switch.
☐ Check for any air leaks from the casing or ducts and seal them by tightening bolts, gaskets, or caulking compound.
☐ Clean or replace the filters on an air furnace.

When the serviceman arrives for the recommended fall tune-up, ask him to check and adjust the following:

☐ Air draft regulator
☐ Oil filter
☐ Spark gap
☐ Air-tube shutter
☐ Transformer
☐ Stack gas analysis and temperature
☐ Air stat or acquastat
☐ Clean the nozzle and change if worn
☐ Oil-air ratio

Warm-Air Systems

Distribution

Balance the air flow to each room in accordance with your needs by adjusting the dampers, which are metal plates inside the ducts. Large ducts connected to the furnace, called *trunk lines,* branch out to smaller ducts, supplying each room. Dampers in the trunk lines permit zoned heating control; dampers in the branch ducts permit individual room control. The dampers may be automatically controlled by the zone or room thermostat. If they are not, you should adjust them manually to deliver heat to the room.

Combustion Air

As your furnace burns it draws in warm indoor air to be reheated. This often causes cold outside air to be pulled into the house through small cracks and openings. Consider adding a small duct to supply outdoor air to the furnace area. The direct supply of combustion air should be tempered—slightly warmed—by letting the air pass over the furnace exhaust stack after it leaves the duct. Ask your serviceman if this adaptation is feasible with your existing equipment layout. If so, it can significantly reduce fuel bills and uncomfortable drafts throughout the house. Do not connect the duct to the furnace.

Registers

You can control the air distribution to each room at the registers. These are the grilles in the wall, floor, or ceiling. They may already have a damper built in. If they don't, it is worthwhile to replace them with adjustable louvers. This is especially cost-effective if the ductwork is not damper controlled. Be sure that the circulation of heated air from the registers is not blocked by furniture or drapes.

Insulation

Warm-air ducts may have been installed without insulation and routed from the furnace or boiler through unheated spaces such as crawl spaces and unheated garages or basements. Without proper insulation a lot of heat will be lost, and extra heating is needed to supply the farthest room with the desired temperatures. Ducts supplying warm air in winter and air conditioning in the summer require insulation with a vapor barrier to prevent condensation. You don't need the vapor barrier to adequately protect ducts supplying warm air only. Building supply centers stock *duct insulation*. You can use these preshaped materials or wrap the ducts with insulating batts or blankets. (See Chart 2 to select the material to provide an insulation value between R-8 and R-11.)

Hot-Water Systems

Distribution

It is more difficult to control heat distribution in a hot-water system than in a forced warm-air system. The pump circulates the heated water from the boiler through pipes to the radiators where the heat is transferred to the surrounding air. You can control the heat supplied to each room with valves on the inlet side of the radiator or with dampers on the convectors. If your home does not have zoned heating with valves in the hot-water lines, use the individual radiator valves to balance the flow of heat.

Hot water baseboard *convectors* have metal fins along the pipe to provide increased heat output per linear foot.

☐ Be sure that no furniture or drapes block the baseboard units because they usually rely on natural air currents to circulate the air in the room.

☐ Your convectors probably have air-vent valves to allow trapped air to escape. If yours do not operate automatically start the pump and open each air vent. Then heat the water and adjust each vent.

☐ Don't paint the radiator silver; it retards the heat transfer to the surrounding air.

☐ Place reflective material on the wall behind the radiator to reflect the heat into the room.

Boiler

Whether the hot-water boiler is heated by gas, oil, or electricity, be sure that your serviceman includes the following items in the fall maintenance service.

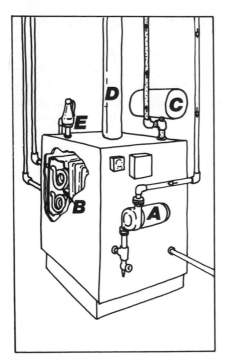

32. In a hot water heating system the water is recirculated through the boiler by pump (A). The boiler also heats domestic water using heat exchange coils (B). Note also, expansion tank (C), exhaust flue (D), and pressure reducing valve (E).

☐ Clean and scrape the fire-side to remove soot and scale.

☐ Clean the water-sides to remove built-up scale.

☐ Check the insulation on the boiler to insure a value of R-10.

☐ Check for air leaks between sections of cast-iron boilers and seal them.

☐ Install baffles or turbulators if the combustion efficiency is at a maximum but the stack temperatures are still too high.

☐ Maintain the lowest possible hot-water temperature which will meet space heating or domestic hot-water needs.

☐ Seal all air leaks into natural draft chimneys, especially where flue pipe enters the wall.

Insulation

All hot-water pipes running through unheated spaces should be insulated. If hot pipes are exposed inside living spaces you should insulate them to prevent accidental skin burns and damage to adjacent materials. You can buy preformed pipe insulation made of fiberglass or foam for easy installation. If you cannot get this type of insulation, be sure that the insulation you buy can withstand the high pipe temperatures and is acceptable to the local fire department.

If you already have some pipe insulation, check its condition and thickness. Where it is loose or incomplete, strip it away and replace it entirely. Where it is very thin and hot to the touch, add new insulation over it.

Add-On Devices

In addition to maintenance and repair tasks, look into the marketplace for devices such as the ones below, which may increase the efficiency of your existing heating system. Check with the serviceman to make sure that it will be compatible with your system before you purchase the device.

Electronic spark ignition systems replace the pilot light on gas furnaces. Many new gas furnaces are now built with this feature to eliminate the continuously wasteful gas pilot.

Flue heat exchangers can capture some of the unused heat which goes up the flue in your oil or gas heating system. They attach onto the flue. The reclaimed heat can be ducted into your existing supply duct, or directly into a room.

Automatic flue dampers prevent the heat in the combustion chamber from escaping up the chimney between the firing cycles of your gas-fired boiler or furnace. It closes the flue 30 seconds after the burners go off and restarts automatically 30 seconds before the next firing cycle.

Electric Resistance Heating

There is very little you can do to increase the operating efficiency of resistance heating for your furnace, boiler, or baseboard units. The generating inefficiencies at the power plant and distribution costs are beyond your control.

In most regions of the country, electric heating bills are high and are rapidly escalating. You should implement a plan to reduce your home's heating requirements. Each energy-conserving measure will be more cost-effective than for oil- or gas-heated homes. You should also refer to Part II for alternative energy sources for home heating.

If electric resistance coils are the heat source for your warm-air system or hot-water system, refer to those sections of this chapter to increase the efficiency of the distribution system.

If you have individual electric baseboard heaters, regulate each one carefully with the built-in thermostatic control. Since the heat is delivered immediately you may be able to keep some units at lower settings much of the time.

Consider the use of *heat pumps.*

Heat Pumps

If electric resistance coils are used in your furnace, consider investing in an energy-efficient heat pump. It can be integrated with your existing warm-air system in much the same way as you might add an air-conditioning unit. The heat pump is powered by electricity far more efficiently than your present electric resistance system and can provide cooling as well as heating. If you are using baseboard electric heating, you can install a unitary air-to-air heat pump and use the baseboard system for supplementary heating.

In simple terms, the heat pump mechanisms absorb heat from one source and release it somewhere else. During cold weather, an air-to-air heat pump extracts heat from the outdoor air, raises its temperature, and delivers it to the house. In the warm weather, the mechanism reverses, extracting heat from the house and releasing it to the outside. (In order to use a water-to-water or water-to-air heat pump you must have a constant water source, such as an underground stream.)

Heat pumps have been widely used in moderate climates since they operate at peak heating efficiency at temperatures about 45°F (7°C). Newer models can be efficiently used in colder climates in conjunction with your resistance heating element, or with an oil- or gas-fired device as a backup.

Heat pumps are sold by many of the heating and cooling equipment manufacturers. Check the installation and service contract prices to figure your total investment. Be sure to select a model with an Energy Efficiency Ratio (EER) of at least 10. These are expensive machines but can reduce your electric heating costs by 50 to 70 percent.

Cooling

In many regions of the United States mechanical air-conditioning equipment is used to reduce the discomfort of excessive heat and humidity. Most air conditioners are powered by electricity and consume 400 kwh or more each month in the cooling season. Home-repair tasks, such as insulating, caulking, weatherstripping, and ventilating, should be implemented to lower the demand on your air-conditioning units and reduce operating costs. On cool nights, open the windows and turn on the attic fan to ventilate your house. (See Chapters 1 and 2.) There are several maintenance procedures you can do at home to increase the operating efficiency of your equipment.

Maintenance

Whether you have room air conditioners or a central air-conditioning system, take the time to do the following tasks as recommended in your owner's manual.

☐ Clean or replace the air filter.
☐ Oil the fan motor.
☐ Clean the condenser coils and the evaporator coils.
☐ In central systems, adjust the dampers from the heating settings to cooling settings. Be sure that all ducts are fully insulated.
☐ Check for the proper refrigerant level annually.
☐ Check for leaks in the refrigerant coil.

Habits

☐ The recommended indoor temperature for normal comfort is 78°F (25°C). Each degree change is worth about 3 percent of your cooling costs.
☐ Adjust the grilles to direct the flow of cool air toward the ceiling to promote efficient circulation.
☐ Where the unit extends outside your window or wall, be sure that the air flow is not obstructed by foliage.

49

☐ Provide an awning to shade the condenser (outside part of the unit) to increase its efficiency by at least 2 percent.

☐ Keep the air conditioner off when no one is at home. It is more economical to install an automatic timer to start the unit a half hour before you get home.

☐ For room units, use the lower fan speeds when the heat and humidity are not extreme.

☐ For room units, keep the outside air damper closed except to remove offensive odors.

☐ For central systems locate the thermostat where it can sense the air circulating from several rooms.

☐ When the weather turns cold be sure to cover the outside of the unit with heavy duty plastic such as 6 mil polyethylene. This will reduce heat loss in the winter and extend the life of the air conditioner.

Buying a Room Air Conditioner

You should carefully examine the space to be cooled before shopping for an air conditioner.

☐ Measure the volume of space—its length, width, and height.

☐ Know the orientation of the exterior wall(s)—north, south, east, and west.

☐ Check the insulation qualities of the space—its ability to resist heat gain and to retain the cooled air.

With this basic information you can get accurate guidance in sizing the unit you need. Air conditioners are rated by their ability to remove a specific number of units of heat (BTU's) each hour. Many people refer to the machine's capacity in *tons;* a 6,000 BTU unit is equivalent to a half ton of cooling capacity.

When you know the size (capacity) unit you need, check carefully to find the unit with the highest Energy Efficiency Ratio (EER). Each air conditioner lists the wattage (electric power) it consumes. The EER defines the relationship between the machine's cooling capacity and its energy usage.

$$EER = \frac{BTU\ Rating}{Wattage}$$

The higher the EER the less it costs to run the unit. For example, a 6,000 BTU unit which requires 800 watts has an EER of 7.5. A more efficient 6,000 BTU model requiring 600 watts has an EER of 10. It is worthwhile to do some comparative shopping to find a room air conditioner with an EER between 9 and 11. Many manufacturers now display the EER ratings in their advertising. The most efficient models are more expensive but insure significantly lower operating costs. The additional cost will be recouped in energy savings during the first year of operation in many regions of the country.

Humidifiers

On a winter day with the room temperature at 72°F (22°C), you may still feel chilled if there is not enough moisture in the air. For year-round comfort, the indoor relative humidity should be between 30 and 50 percent. (You should measure the relative humidity with a *hygrometer*.) Use a humidifier to maintain this level in the winter and you will be more comfortable at lower house temperatures. Turning down the thermostat often saves more on the heating bill than it costs to operate the humidifier. If your house has a lot of leaks and cracks, be sure to apply caulking, weatherstripping, and vapor barriers. (See Chapter 2.) Also, in the cold weather, operate your kitchen and bathroom exhaust fans as little as necessary; they will expel the moisture and heat as well as the odors and smoke.

In regions where you have high summer temperatures and high relative humidity, the moisture in the air adds to your discomfort. Air conditioners act as dehumidifiers by drawing the moisture from the house and expelling it in the form of condensation. Running your air conditioner at low speeds results in more efficient dehumidification.

Equipment

☐ The easiest temporary method of supplying moisture vapor is to place a pan of water near the room's heat source—radiator, fireplace, or stove. Refill the water as it evaporates.

☐ Portable humidifers are sold as tabletop models or freestanding floor units, which plug into an ordinary wall outlet. You add the water which is either sprayed as a fine mist into the air (atomizer type) or picked up by warm air blown into the room through a wet mat (evaporator type).

☐ If you have a central forced warm-air heating system, you can

51

add a humidifier with the help of a trained installer. This will add moisture to the air whenever the heat is circulated.

In automatically operating humidifiers, a built-in device called a *humidistat* senses and controls the humidity at the desired level. The humidifiers are capable of delivering between a half gallon and two gallons of water per day to each room in your house. The capacity you need depends on the weathertightness of the house and the outside temperature and humidity conditions.

Water Heating

Your water-heating tank consumes gas, oil, or electricity and stores the water at a set temperature. The energy cost for water heating can amount to 20 percent of your total monthly fuel bill. (See Chapter 5.)

This section suggests opportunities to increase the efficiency of your water-heating equipment.

Thermostat

Many water heaters are set on the "high" reading of 145°F (63°C) to 165°F (92°C), far above the temperatures you actually need. Normal household use requires hot water at 110°F (43°C), so adjust the thermostat to "medium" and test the results. If your thermostat has temperature set points, try the setting at 110° or lower until you find the water is just hot enough. Each degree reduction saves energy. Dishwashers do require 140°F (60°C) water. If yours does not have a booster heater, it pays to have one installed on the dishwasher supply line and keep the bulk of stored water at 110°F. If you are replacing the dishwasher, many newer models have the boosters built in.

Insulation

Your water heater's label may indicate "insulated," but if the heater is warm to the touch, it is still wasting heat and should be insulated further. You can wrap the tank with fiberglass batts or buy packaged kits to fit easily over water heaters of different sizes. Be sure that in either case the insulation has a value of R-11. When you do the installation be careful not to cover the combustion air intake openings on the surface of the tank.

The hot water pipes should be insulated to a value of R-8. You can use the methods suggested for pipe insulation on page 62. Insulating the tank and pipes can cut the energy for water heating by 15 percent.

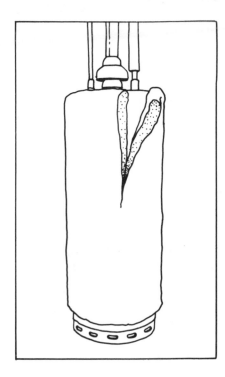

33. Insulate your domestic water heater with conventional fiberglass blankets or a packaged insulating jacket.

Sediment

Your water heater, unlike a space-heating boiler, operates all year long. You should drain out the sediment every three or four months. The sediment builds up in the bottom of the tank forming a barrier between the heating element and the water. Open the tap near the bottom of the tank and let the water drain into a bucket until it runs clear.

Recommendations

☐ On gas-fired water heaters, have your serviceman replace the pilot light with an electronic spark ignition device.

☐ If you are burdened with an electric water heater and pay more than 4¢ per kwh, you should investigate solar water heating systems. (See Chapter 6.)

☐ If your water is heated in an exterior tankless coil or one passing through the space-heating tank, you should have it replaced with a separate gas, oil, or solar water heater. You are inefficiently operating the large boiler to supply hot water at times when space heating is not required.

□ If you are buying new equipment, your choice of a gas- or oil-fired water heater depends on the local fuel costs and availability. It is worthwhile to buy an energy-saving model with a ten-year warranty. These models are more expensive but the extra initial cost will be offset by the energy savings in the first year or two of operation. For the next ten to fifteen years, you will be spending less on water-heating bills every month.

Lighting

If you use no electricity for home heating, air conditioning, or water heating, the lighting accounts for 20 to 25 percent of your monthly electric bill, with household appliances consuming the rest. You can reduce the electricity used for lighting by replacing inefficient products and wasteful habits.

Products

Incandescent bulbs are like miniature electric resistance heaters. In fact, 90 percent of the energy consumed is given off as heat, while 10 percent of the energy produces light. The amount of electricity the bulb uses is measured in *watts* and the amount of light produced is measured in *lumens*. No matter what kind of bulb you are buying, you want the most light for the least electricity. Use the ratings printed on the bulb package to do the following calculation:

$$\text{Bulb Efficiency} = \frac{\text{Lumens}}{\text{Watts}}$$

Another rating listed on the bulb package is the *bulb life* which is an estimate of the number of hours the bulb will burn. This number has little bearing on the efficiency of the bulb but will assist you in choosing bulbs for hard-to-reach areas in your home.

Long-life incandescents are specially designed to yield less light than a standard bulb of the same wattage; but they last longer and ultimately produce the same amount of light and consume the same wattage. They are not energy savers, and you should use them only where replacement is difficult.

Three-way bulbs enable you to adjust the light level on table and floor lamps with appropriate sockets. You can generally use the lowest setting to save electricity and turn it up only when you need the higher lighting. They are available in preset combinations such as 30/70/100 and 50/100/150 watts.

Dimmers are rotating or sliding switches which enable you to control the brightness of any incandescent lighting fixture. (Dimmers for fluorescent fixtures are too expensive to be cost-effective energy savers.) You can easily replace standard light switches with dimmers to lower the lighting level, reduce the wattage, and extend the bulb life. Hardware stores carry many models of dimmers which cost about five dollars.

For wall switches, simply shut off the power to the circuit, remove the switch plate and the old switch, then disconnect the two wires and reconnect them to the dimmer.

For table lamps and floor lamps, install a portable dimmer which plugs into the wall outlet and receives the lamp plug. You can splice in a dimmer along the cord between the lamp and the outlet. Be sure to first unplug the lamp.

Special sockets are available with built-in dimmers to replace a conventional brass lamp socket.

Fluorescent tubes operate by an *electric discharge* method, which is far more efficient than the resistance method of incandescent bulbs.

- [ ] They produce 4 to 10 times more lumens per watt.
- [ ] They last 10 to 15 times longer.
- [ ] They give off less heat for the same unit of light.
- [ ] Longer fluorescent tubes are more efficient than shorter ones.
- [ ] U-shaped tubes are even more efficient than straight ones.

You probably will not want to have fluorescent tubes lighting the whole house despite their efficiency. But you should consider using cool or warm white tubes where color rendition and aesthetics are not essential, such as your garage, work area, mechanical room, or unfinished basement. When recessed in lighting coves, flourescents can produce a soft, evenly distributed light, especially the "Deluxe Color" tubes.

If you want to replace existing incandescent fixtures with fluorescent tubes, you must use special adapters available at hardware or electric supply stores.

Habits

- [ ] Turning off lights saves energy, but frequent switching shortens the bulb life. If you will be out of the room for more than five minutes, it pays to turn off the lights—even fluorescents which require more electricity to get started.

☐ Look at your lighting level throughout the house. Wherever it can be comfortably reduced, replace the bulbs with lower wattage bulbs. Closets and hallways are good examples.

☐ If you need high-level general lighting, replace several bulbs with fewer high wattage bulbs. One 100-watt bulb produces the same amount of light as two 60-watt bulbs and uses 20 percent less electricity (see Chart 4).

————————————Chart 4————————————

Incandescent			Straight Fluorescent			
Watts	Lumens	Life*	Watts**	Lumens Standard Colors	Lumens Deluxe Colors	Life*
25 W	235	2500 hrs.	14 W	700	470	9000 hrs.
40 W	455	1500	15 W	870	600	9000
60 W	870	1000	20 W	1300	850	9000
75 W	1190	1000	30 W	2360	1530	18000
100 W	1750	1000	40 W	3150	2200	20000
150 W	2880	1000				
200 W	4010	1000				

*Average rated life.   **Nominal lamp watts.

☐ For reading, sewing, or writing use localized high-level lighting, *task lighting,* and lower the general lighting level.

☐ If you have outdoor security lighting, replace incandescents with HID mercury vapor lights which last about fifteen times longer. Also, install an automatic timer control.

☐ For safety, never leave a live socket empty. Fill it with a burned-out bulb.

☐ Dust and dirt on bulbs, reflectors, and lampshades can reduce lighting efficiency by 50 percent.

☐ Take advantage of daylight through windows and skylights. Keep in mind that summer heat gain will increase air-conditioning loads and winter heat gain on southern exposures will reduce heating loads. (see Chapter 2.)

☐ Install small indicator lights in the living space to signal for any lights left burning in unoccupied spaces. The wiring is simple and inexpensive compared to the cost of continuous, unnecessary lighting.

☐ If you are repainting your home, light colors reflect more light than dark colors and enable you to reduce the necessary wattage for the light you want.

Further Reading

1. Editors of Consumer Guide, *Energy Savers Catalog,* New York: G. P. Putnam and Sons, 1977.

A guide to available products for energy efficient mechanical and electrical equipment.

2. Fred S. Dubin, *Life Support Systems for a Dying Planet,* special issue of Progressive Architecture, Stamford, Conn. October 1971.

3. M. David Egan, *Concepts in Thermal Comfort,* Engelwood Cliffs, N.J.: Prentice-Hall Inc., 1975.

4

HOUSEHOLD APPLIANCES

Without electric heating, air conditioning, or water heating, the running of your major appliances may account for 75 percent of your monthly electric bill. Careful choice and use of these machines can cut their energy consumption by 15 to 30 percent. Chart 5 lists your major household appliances and their monthly energy needs. These figures reflect industry estimates of gas and electricity use by conventional appliances.

How much do you pay to run your major appliances each month? Do a quick appliance count, then call your utility company and find out what you are paying for each kilowatt hour (electricity) and therm (gas) you buy. Calculate your appliance costs with Chart 5, as follows:

$$\text{Estimated Monthly Energy Use of Appliance} \times \text{Cost per Unit of Energy} = \text{Cost to Run Appliance Each Month}$$

Example:

Freezer: 150 kwh   × 4¢ per kwh   = $6 to run freezer
each month

Add up the monthly costs for every major appliance you use. Energy-efficient appliances are now available with features that will use fewer of your energy dollars per month. When you look for replacements, shop for these models. The salesperson can tell you the monthly energy consumption of different models which you can compare with Chart 5. Remember, a machine that costs fifty dollars more to buy today may save you two hundred dollars in operating costs during its lifetime. So make all the necessary calculations on pay-back opportunities before investing in any new appliance.

Energy savings are possible even with older, conventional appliances. Good maintenance and personal habits will help you conserve, rather than waste, your appliance energy dollars.

Energy Peak Load

The time of day when you run your appliances is important. During the peak periods of the day, the electric utility companies have to use

———————————Chart 5———————————

Your Major Household Appliances

Household Energy Consumption in Kilowatt-Hours and Therms	Estimated Monthly Energy Use
Refrigerator	
Manual Defrost, 10 cubic feet	60 kwh
Partial Automatic Defrost, 12 cubic feet	90 kwh
Frostless, 16 cubic feet	250 kwh
Frostless, 20 cubic feet	300 kwh
Freezer	
Frostless, 15 cubic feet	150 kwh
Range and Oven (three meals per day)	
Electrical Range and Oven	150 kwh
Gas Range and Oven with Pilot Light	15 therms
Gas Range and Oven without Pilot Light	9 therms
Clothes Washer (one load per day, 50 gallons)	
Electrical Consumption for Motor	8 kwh
Electrical Consumption for Hot Water @ 140° F	190 kwh
Gas Consumption for Hot Water @ 140° F	5 therms
Clothes Dryer (one load per day)	
Electric Clothes Dryer	100 kwh
Gas Clothes Dryer with Pilot Light	10 therms + 8 kwh
Gas Clothes Dryer without Pilot Light	5 therms + 8 kwh
Dishwasher (one load per day, 15 gallons)	
Electricity for Motor	30 kwh
Electrical Consumption for Hot Water @ 140° F	90 kwh
Gas Consumption for Hot Water @ 140° F	5 therms
Microwave Oven (three 5-minute uses per day)	
Electrical Oven	9 kwh
Oven Self-Cleaning Feature (one use per month)	
Electrical Oven	6 kwh
Gas Oven	½ therm

expensive and inefficient backup equipment to meet the heavy energy demand. Use of your major appliances during the early morning or late evening will help reduce this peak load and energy waste. The energy saved will not be noted on your electric bill unless you install a special or separate meter authorized by your utility company. Call your utility company to inquire about the discount rates. Even if you cannot get a rate reduction, avoid early evening use (6:00-9:00 P.M.) during the winter and afternoon use (12:00-6:00 P.M.) during the summer. Your personal effort will help reduce the need for future generating facilities.

Knowing Your Appliances

Any time you purchase a new appliance you should read the operating manual. Familiarity with its maintenance needs will help you understand how to properly clean and care for it. Even if you purchase a used appliance, or if your home was built appliance-equipped, you may save yourself future servicing if you write to the manufacturer for a new manual.

Refrigerators and Freezers

Running on a twenty-four-hour schedule, refrigerators and freezers consume the biggest chunk of your appliance-operating costs. Refrigerators and freezers should be selected with overall size, insulation, and method of defrosting in mind.

Key Features

Insulation. Poor insulation is the major design flaw in conventional refrigerators and freezers. Although some manufacturers have begun to use polyfoam insulation, they have also decreased the wall thickness to create a larger interior. There are usually no energy savings for you. Look for increased insulation in any new unit you purchase.

Good Features. When buying a combination refrigerator and freezer unit, look for:

☐ Separate doors for both freezer and refrigerator compartments and controls that are easily accessible.
☐ A top- or bottom-mounted freezer instead of a side-mounted one.
☐ Castors and removable grille for easy cleaning of the condensor coils
☐ A power-saving switch which turns off the electric *heat strips.* (These auxiliary, low-wattage heaters are normally located inside the

refrigerator and freezer door panels and the dividing section between them. They prevent condensation on the cabinet exterior. These heaters are most useful during humid weather and should be turned off when the unit is less likely to "sweat.")

Inefficient Features. If you decide to invest the extra money in a frost-free unit, be prepared to continue to pay for its convenience. The defrosting mechanism adds roughtly 50 percent more to your operating costs.

Look out for such options as ice makers, water coolers, and refreshment dispensers. Every new mechanism adds to your operating costs and future repair bills.

Maintenance

Placement. Locate your refrigerator in the coolest part of your kitchen. If it is presently near any heat source, such as a stove or radiator, either move the unit or put a noncombustible insulating material between it and the heat source. Direct sunlight or placement against an uninsulated wall should also be avoided.

Ventilation. Your refrigerator needs room to ventilate. In particular, a frost-free model must have air to evaporate its constant supply of defrosted water. Leave a 2- to 3-inch clearance around your refrigerator's exterior when you place it in your kitchen.

Door Seal. Warm air will seep into your refrigerator or freezer if the gasket around the doors is worn or damaged. Air seepage is most obvious in manual defrost units where fluffy, snowlike ice forms in and around the freezer section. To test the gaskets, place a dollar bill between the gasket and the cabinet. After closing the door, try to pull the dollar bill straight out. A definite resistance should be felt as you remove the bill. Try this test all around the door, including the hinge side. If you discover a poor seal or misalignment of the door to the cabinet, try the following suggestions:

1. Check to see if your refrigerator or freezer is level. Poor cabinet-to-door alignment will result if the unit is tilted. There are usually threaded feet that can be adjusted for proper leveling.
2. Try washing the gasket with warm water and mild soap to remove any food particles or debris which may be stuck in the gasket.
3. Check the door latch to see if it needs an adjustment. Rather than risk permanent damage, call a handyman to fix it.
4. Check door-to-cabinet alignment if the gasket is not sealing in certain spots. Loosen the screws for the inner door panel and twist

gently until it flexes to the desired alignment. Tighten the screws.

5. If all else fails, you probably need to replace your gasket. Your refrigerator age and size determine the cost for a gasket replacement. If your model has an old-fashioned catch mechanism, the gasket should cost around twenty-two dollars. If the doors close magnetically the gasket is lined with magnets and costs about thirty five dollars. Installing a new gasket on an older refrigerator or freezer usually requires removal of the door panel. On newer models the gasket is screwed onto a retaining band. To install the new gasket, unscrew the old one and carefully screw in the new one. A magnetic gasket may need to be gently heated to straighten out kinks during installation. Use a hair dryer at a low setting. You will probably have to adjust the door hinges after you complete the job. (Replacement gaskets usually take one to two weeks of use before sealing properly.)

Defrosting

Every refrigerator should be defrosted before any frost becomes ¼-inch thick and overworks the compressor.

A *Manual Defrost Refrigerator* needs to be defrosted frequently—probably every one to six weeks depending on whether you have a single or double-door model and how often you open the doors. (A manual defrost model loses all of its energy-efficient qualities once its insides are caked with ice.)

A *Cycle Defrost Refrigerator* has a separate freezer which needs to be defrosted manually three to four times a year while the refrigerator section defrosts automatically. This feature is probably the most efficient if you can't defrost regularly.

A *Frost-Free Refrigerator* automatically defrosts both the freezer and refrigerator sections but is not recommended for the reasons stated under Key Features.

The best procedure for defrosting your refrigerator or freezer is as follows:

1. Turn the dial to defrost or, to the "off" position, or unplug the unit.

2. Remove all contents, making sure to wrap frozen foods in news-paper bundles to keep them from thawing.

3. Place pans inside the freezer and partially fill with boiling water. As the ice melts into the pans, remove and drain. Repeat the procedure until all of the ice has been removed from the freezer compartment. It is important *not* to pick at the ice with any sharp objects as you may puncture one of the coolant tubes which could result in an expensive repair bill.

4. Once the refrigerator and freezer are ice-free, dial the controls back to the correct setting (or plug in).

Cleaning

Condensor Coils. All models have condensor coils located either on the back or bottom of the box. These coils dispose of the heat that is removed from the refrigerated spaces and they must be kept clean and unobstructed. Often you must move the refrigerator to get to the coils, which is why casters are recommended. If the coils are on the back of the refrigerator, clean them with an ammonia-soaked cloth. Otherwise, they are under the refrigerator and you will need to use a vacuum cleaner with an appropriate attachment. In any case, you should clean your condensor once every three months. If you only clean once a year, save this job for the beginning of the summer season.

Condensate Drains. All frost-free refrigerators have drains that lead the defrosted water out of the refrigerator unit onto a tray under the box. Check your operating manual for its specific location and then make sure that it is kept empty and clean at all times.

Toe Grille. Many models of refrigerators have a toe grille on the front of the appliance. If you clean this grille periodically, the improved air circulation will aid in the necessary ventilation.

Interior. Even cleaning the inside of your refrigerator will help maintain its efficiency. Include this chore while you are defrosting and the appliance is already turned off.

Temperature

The temperature settings in your refrigerator and freezer dictate their energy consumption. Obviously, the colder the setting, the more energy is required to maintain that temperature.

In an older manual defrost refrigerator, the freezer is within the box and the temperature ranges from 10°F (-12°C) 20°F (-7°C). All frozen foods should be consumed within two or three weeks of freezing for guaranteed freshness.

Food frozen at 0°F (-18°C) can be stored for up to a year, otherwise 5°F (-15°C) is cold enough for your short-term freezing needs.

It is best to check your refrigeration temperatures using a thermometer to make sure the settings aren't too cold for your needs.

Usually, refrigerators are coldest at the back of the top shelf. This is the best place to store your most perishable foods while maintaining your refrigerator at a higher temperature.

Power Saver Switch. Most new refrigerators have a power saver switch located inside the box near the temperature control. As mentioned earlier, this control can be used to turn off the heat strips. Using this switch on all but the muggiest of days will save you 16 percent of your energy costs.

Extension Cords. You shouldn't connect your refrigerator or freezer via a normal extension cord. The added length of small gauge wire increases the amount of electricity needed to supply your refrigeration unit. Use a heavy duty extension sold for large appliances.

Habits

Door Opening

The average duration of a refrigerator- or freezer-door opening (12 seconds) is just long enough to cause a 100 percent air change. Obviously, the number and duration of door openings should be minimized to reduce loss of the cold air. This is probably the most energy-efficient habit that you can be aware of.

Loading

Loading your refrigerator properly will help minimize its energy useage.

In the refrigerator, cool air must be able to circulate around each food item. Place the containers slightly apart and try not to overload the shelves. However, the freezer section should be tightly packed (with ice cubes if necessary). It is easier to maintain stored food at constant cold temperatures than it is to bring the remaining air space down to the required low temperature.

Removing excess packaging (which acts as an insulation barrier rather than a moisture seal) will help bring the food to its desired temperature faster.

Freezing food requires more energy than refrigerating it. If you plan on using up a food item quickly, store it in the refrigerator section.

Frozen foods, while thawing, can help keep your refrigerator cold. Place frozen food in the refrigerator the night before you need it and it will be thawed in time for dinner.

Covering all food containers will reduce the moisture content inside the refrigerator and lessen the electrical work load, especially in frost-free models.

Cooling hot foods before placing them in the refrigerator or freezer will reduce the temperature loss inside the box. To prevent bacterial growth, it is best to leave food at room temperature for no more than twenty minutes.

Do not freeze more than 2 or 3 pounds of food per cubic foot of freezer space within a twenty-four-hour period. You will strain the appliance.

Leaving Your Refrigerator

If you are leaving home for even a week, it is best to remove all perishable foods from your refrigerator. Place an open box of baking soda inside, then prop open the door after turning it off or turn the temperature control to a warmer setting to offset the lack of door openings and air changes.

Ranges

Key Features

Electric Ignition on Gas Appliances. A gas range should only be purchased with an electric ignition switch. Pilot lights consume one-third of the gas used by your unit while serving no useful heating purpose.

Insulation. The best insulated models are designed with the self-cleaning feature. Using the self-cleaning device is wasteful of energy, but the high insulating value can save 20 percent of your operating costs.

Oven Window. A window in your oven door cuts down on your insulation. The bigger the window, the greater the heat loss. However, if you are a worrier or a peeker, each door opening drops your oven temperature by 25 percent which may well justify a small window and oven light.

Electric Burners. Thermostatically controlled burners are energy savers which do not require a constant supply of electricity when in use. It is also possible to get a power saver unit which regulates the amount of heat given off by the burner according to the diameter of the pan you use.

Oven Cleaning

Pyrolitic Self-Cleaning. This cleaning cycle is a cremation process for any food residue coated inside the oven. It requires a well-insulated appliance and takes from one and one-half to three hours to complete. You should use this feature sparingly, with the timer set for the minimum duration, and only after the oven has already been used and heated up. On the average, the self-cleaning process will use 72 kwh per year.

Continuous Cleaning. A continuous-cleaning oven does not consume any extra energy to do the job. It is simply a specially treated coating inside the oven upon which the residue is gradually reduced during baking. Because this type of stove has normal insulating capabilities, it is not as efficient as the self-cleaning model.

Models Available

Programmed Ovens. New models feature a clock which is integrated with the oven control to achieve a "cook-and-hold" cycle and a "delay-cook-hold" cycle. After the food has cooked, both cycles automatically lower the oven temperature to a "keep-warm" setting until serving time. The only advantage to the "keep-warm" setting is that it uses less energy in one hour than you would need to reheat the same food to serving temperature.

Forced-Air Ovens. Forced-air ovens use a concealed fan to direct the oven's heat in a constant flow throughout the oven and use substantially less time and energy than a conventional oven.

Microwave Oven. A microwave oven uses 30 to 70 percent *less* energy than a conventional oven when reheating, defrosting, or cooking in small quantities. Manufacturers now sell freestanding ranges with combination microwave/conventional features in a single oven. This combination seems the most versatile for the average kitchen. Although microwave ovens offer good energy savings, you should also consider possible health hazards resulting from improper use. (Especially if a member of your family or a friend has a heart pacemaker.)

Ceramic Cooktops. Ranges with ceramic cooking surfaces require about 15 percent *more* energy than regular electric tops because the intervening layer of ceramic between the element and the pan must also be heated up. Their attractive surfaces require constant cleaning.

Maintenance

Oven Cleaning. A simple and effective way to clean your oven is to place a bowl of ammonia in the closed oven overnight. By morning, the fumes will have loosened the grease and grime and the task can be completed with soap and water. Commercial cleaning products are available but with this method you can avoid using aerosol-spray products.

Sealing. Periodically check the gasket around your oven door, using the dollar-bill trick explained under refrigerator maintenance. Clean the gasket regularly, and if necessary, replace the seal to minimize heat loss.

Range Cleaning. Keep the burners on your range clean by washing the bowls and drip pans in sudsy water and allowing them to dry thoroughly. Keep your burner pans clean and shiny for good reflection of heat and you can increase the efficiency of your electric unit by 30 percent. On gas ranges, remove the burner heads, wash and dry, but make sure you replace them securely.

Gas Flame. If you have a gas range, make sure your pilot is burning efficiently with a blue flame. If the flame is yellowish it indicates an adjustment is needed. Call your utility company to see if they offer free servicing, but get the adjustment made. Your pilot light consumes 30 percent of your range's energy needs.

Habits

Your Stove

Aluminum and copper pots are good conductors and spread heat evenly. Stainless steel is good in combination with an aluminum or copper bottom. Cast iron is slow to heat up because of its thickness but is well suited for long cooking jobs.

Use flat-bottomed pans with close-fitting covers for best thermal transfer and retention of steam heat. Keep the lid on.

Match the size of your pan to the burner, especially with an electric range. If you cook with electric heat, turn the element off five minutes early and let the heat remaining in the unit finish the job.

Use the minimum amount of water necessary, especially when cooking vegetables. Kettles are good containers for boiling water, but don't fill them up unless you need all of the boiled water.

Try to cook one-dish meals often or to steam several foods at once.

Thaw frozen foods in the refrigerator before you need to cook them.

Use a pressure cooker to reduce cooking time whenever possible.

Your Oven

Because your oven is thermostatically controlled, it is efficient when used to its maximum capacity or for long cooking jobs.

Before turning your oven on, arrange the shelves. Place the cookware so they don't touch the walls or each other and are not directly above one another.

If you must preheat, 10 minutes is ample time. Preheating requires 2 to 28 percent more energy than baking from a cold start.

Glass or ceramic cookware give better heat transfer than metals. If you use them in your oven, turn the thermostat 25 percent below the recommended temperature in the recipe instructions.

Each time you open your oven door to peek, the oven temperature drops 25 to 50°, depending on the duration of your survey.

Turn off your oven five minutes before the total cooking time of a short baking job. The heat retained in the oven will finish the job, if you keep the door closed. If you have had the oven on for several hours, you can turn it off much earlier, and there will be enough heat to finish the roast.

Never use your oven to heat your kitchen. It is inefficient, and dangerous (especially with gas ovens).

Your broiler uses about 50 percent more fuel than cooking on top of the stove, and 10 percent more than baking in the oven. Use it wisely and sparingly.

Clothes Washer

Your clothes washer consumes 90 percent of its energy for hot water and the additional 10 percent is used by the motor. Using an average of 50 gallons of hot water for the normal cycle, your clothes washer requires almost as much energy per year as your refrigerator.

Key Features

Temperature Selection. Since hot water is the energy culprit for washing machines, it is important to be able to wash in either hot, warm, or cold water and to rinse in only cold water. Cold-water washing is sufficient for two out of three of your washes, offering you 66 percent savings on your hot-water costs. On some models, getting a cold rinse is only possible by resetting the temperature control after the wash cycle. If the control is not reset, the washer will rinse with warm water. Check to make sure an automatic cold rinse cycle is included.

Adjustable Water Level. Optional water levels help you to eliminate full tubs of water when you want to do only a small washing load.

Suds Saver/Water Saver. This feature allows the water to be reused after the second or third rinse. A suds saver model generally costs ten to twenty dollars more and must be used with an adjacent laundry tub. It will save 20 gallons of water per load.

Time Selection. Being able to dial a shorter washing cycle is a boon, especially if the clothes are not too soiled. Cutting the wash cycle from fifteen minutes to eight can save 25 percent of the energy needed to run your motor.

Total Water Savings. Some washing machines are more water conserving than others. Investigating the water needs in proportion to the tub size will tell you how much clothing you can do for how much water. Obviously the less water you use, the less water you need to heat up.

Spin-Dry. Less energy will be used by your dryer if your washer provides a high-speed spin after a slow-speed wash. In most machines the washer will usually complete a high-speed spin automatically.

Models

Front Loading. Front-loading models use less water and clean the clothes with a revolving cylinder which keeps the clothing constantly tumbling. Depending upon the size of the load, you can save up to 36 percent more water than with a top-loading model and even more of your detergent and bleach.

Top Loading. This type of washer cleans the clothes by use of an agitator or pulsator which churns the clothing around and usually achieves better cleaning.

Portable Washer and Dryer. These portable units are available with some of the features of the larger models. They are best suited for a small family or in crowded quarters and are not especially energy efficient.

Maintenance

Placement. Locate your clothes washer as close to your hot-water heater as possible. This will reduce the distance the hot water must travel and minimize the heat loss in the pipes.

Leveling. Make sure that your washer is level or you will put unnecessary strain on the motor.

Filter Cleaning. Clean the lint from your filter (if your washer has a filter) as often as recommended by the manufacturer. In cases where your filter is a "bed of nails" type, it is best to clean when the lint is still damp and easy to remove.

Habits

Cold Washing. Eliminating all but the most necessary hot-water washings will save you the most energy and money. Cold-water washings are effective for all but the dirtiest clothes. You may prefer to clean your baby's diapers or the clothing of an ill member of your family in hot water.

Cold Water Detergent. For cold water washing, it is necessary to use the proper soap or detergent. In some parts of the country where detergents are banned, cold-water soap should first be completely dissolved in warm water and then added to your wash. If your cold water is 50°F (10°C) or 60°F (16°C), the soap may not be as effective and you should try washing with warm water and rinsing with cold. In any case, use biodegradable products and read the label on your soap box; oversudsing will not clean the clothes better but will overwork the machine and may require an extra rinse to remove the soap.

Loading. Save your laundry until you have enough for a full load. Your washer uses the same amount of energy for a full load as for a single item and several small loads is wasteful. If you must do a small load, set the water level to a lower setting. If your washer doesn't have a partial-load setting, fill the machine half full and turn the manual dial to the wash setting. Mixing the size of the garments in a full load improves the cleaning action of your washer by allowing freer circulation.

Soaking. If you have oily clothes, it is best to presoak or to use the "soak" cycle on your machine. To presoak heavily soiled clothes, place them in your washer, turn on, and add soap. Once all the water has entered the machine, turn it off for 10 to 15 minutes. After the clothes have had this initial soaking, you can turn on the washing action and let the cycle continue as usual.

Clothes Dryer

Your dryer evaporates the moisture out of your clothes with a heating element, while tumbling them dry to minimize wrinkling. It may be electric or gas, top or front loading.

Key Features

Electric Ignition. A gas dryer with an electric ignition instead of a standing pilot light will save you one-third of your operating costs.

Automatic Temperature or Electronic Control. Both of these controls accurately sense when the wet clothing has reached the desired dryness. Either one will be helpful in preventing unnecessary overdrying and can save you 10 to 15 percent of the energy wasted due to incorrect settings of the timer.

Dryer Size. The amount of energy required to run a small dryer for two separate loads is greater than that required to run one load of the same amount of clothes in a larger dryer.

No-Heat Dry Cycle. This feature allows your most delicate garments to be tumble-dried without use of the heating element.

Maintenance

Placement. Locate your dryer where it is both warm and dry. Humid air circulating through your dryer, or cold air infiltrating its insulation will lengthen drying time and increase the dryer's work load.

Venting. Manufacturers recommend that you vent your dryer to the outside air. This is a good practice in the summer when you don't want the extra heat or moisture entering your house. In the winter, when the heat and humidity are welcome, you can vent your dryer into your home (gas dryers must always be vented to the outside). Install a bypass damper in the exhaust piping and use a rubber band to secure a lint bag or nylon stocking over the opening. At all times, it is important that you remember to keep your exhaust filter clean. Regular removal of collected lint and dust will keep your dryer running efficiently.

Lint Filter. To maximize drying time and maintain full air flow, clean out your lint filter each time you use your dryer.

Cleaning. Vacuum lint and dust from motor housing every three or four months.

Habits

Clothesline. Use your clothesline on warm, sunny days.

Loading. Always fill but do not overload your dryer. Sort your clothes to be dried into heavy and light loads. Then load your dryer with the most difficult drying job. Once the dryer has heated up and completed this task, continue to load it with the heavier items first. If you leave the lightweight items for the last load, you may be able to dry them with the heat retained in the dryer from the earlier loads.

Settings and Controls. If your dryer has an automatic sensor control, use it all the time. Overdrying your clothes by inaccurate timing wears out the fabrics while wasting energy. Also, use your temperature settings at the lowest temperature possible for adequate drying of your clothing.

Drying Time. Many of your garmets do not have to be completely dried before removal from the dryer. To avoid wrinkling natural fibers, such as cotton and wool, make sure they are moist when removed. If you plan to iron clothes later, remove them from the dryer when they are still slightly damp.

Dishwasher

Your dishwasher uses 15 gallons of hot water per load. It is an energy-efficient machine if you use it only when full, and not more than once a day (preferably less). In fact, conscientious use of your dishwasher uses *less hot* water than washing and rinsing your dishes after each meal.

Key Features

Energy-Saving Switch. An energy-saving switch automatically cancels the heat drying cycle and saves 40 to 50 percent of your electrical energy costs.

Insulation. A well-insulated dishwasher will cut heat loss and noise levels during the washing and drying cycles.

Short-Wash Feature. A "short-wash" cycle uses one-third less water than normal cycles and can be used for all but the dirtiest dishes.

Booster Heater. Most dishwashers are equipped with a booster heater which raises the temperature of the incoming water. The heater is slow and takes about one minute for every degree it "boosts" the water. If your domestic hot water supply is set below 140°F (60°C), this is an efficient and necessary device.

Maintenance

Filters. Check the filter screens frequently to make sure they aren't full of food debris.

Cleaning. Occasional cleaning of the inside of your dishwasher will improve its efficiency.

Habits

Loading. Fill but don't overload your dishwasher. Be sure that you load the dishwasher correctly and do not block the detergent dispenser or spray arms.

Rinsing. Rinse the dishes in a dishpan of cold water before placing them in your dishwasher. This is more efficient than the "rinse-hold" cycle which uses 3 to 7 gallons of hot water each time you use it.

Operating. Use the shortest cycle possible to clean your dishes and let them air dry.

Detergent. Use only dishwasher detergents which produce little or no suds. Detergents not meant for dishwashers are ineffective cleaners and may cause your dishwasher to overflow. Measure the detergent accurately.

Water Temperature. The temperature of the dishwashing water should be 140° to dissolve the detergent and kill bacteria. If your machine has no booster heater you can add one and reduce the domestic hot water supply temperature for the rest of your hot water needs.

Plate Warming. Dishwashers should not be used as plate warmers. You will save energy by using the stored heat in your oven for such purposes.

Drying. If your dishwasher does not have an automatic air-dry feature, listen to its internal noises. When you know all the wash and rinse cycles are completed, turn it off and open up the door.

Miscellaneous Appliances

The average American household owns thirty small appliances. Chart 6 lists a variety of miscellaneous appliances. The appliances with resistance coils, such as an iron or electric heater, draw the most electricity and should be used as little as possible. Study Chart 6 to see where you can reduce energy waste.

Small Kitchen Appliances

When you are preparing smaller meals, the use of appliances such as an electric frying pan, toaster-oven, etc., will *save* you energy. It is best to keep these appliances out of drafts when they are in operation.

Television

Color television sets consume 33 percent more energy than black-and-white sets and solid-state are cheaper to run than the tube types. The "instant-on" televisions use electricity twenty-four hours a day to keep their components heated and ready for instant operation. The best method of eliminating the instant-on feature is either to plug into a wall outlet that you can control by a switch or to purchase an approved extension cord with a built-in switch. You can also purchase a timer to attach to your set which will save you energy if you like to nap while watching.

Iron

To minimize your ironing load, follow the instructions in the Clothes Dryer section. Before you are completely through you should turn the iron off and use the stored energy to complete the job. Hanging wrinkled clothing in the bathroom while you are taking a steamy shower will also remove the wrinkles.

74

---Chart 6---

Miscellaneous Electrical Appliances

Appliance	Estimated Energy Consumption
Blender	1/200 kwh per use
Broiler, Portable	1½ kwh per use
Clock	2 kwh per month
Coffee Maker	¼ kwh per brew
Deep Fryer	1 kwh per hour
Electric Blanket—Twin	½ kwh per night
Queen	¾ kwh per night
King	1 kwh per night
Floor Polisher	⅓ kwh per hour
Frying Pan	½ kwh per hour
Hair Dryer (375-watt)	2/5 kwh per hour
Hand Mixer	1/65 kwh per use
Portable Heater (1,500-watt)	1½ kwh per hour
Radio*	1/10 kwh per hour
Record Player*	1/10 kwh per hour
Steam Iron	⅓ kwh per hour
Television*—Black and White	¼ kwh per hour
Color	⅓ kwh per hour
Instant-On	4 to 43 kwh per month
Toaster (two-slice)	1/20 kwh per use
Toaster-Oven, Portable	½ kwh per use
Trash Compactor	1/100 kwh per load
Vacuum Cleaner	½ kwh per hour
Waffle Iron	⅓ kwh per use
Waste Disposer	1/100 kwh per load

*Solid-state equipment uses less electricity per hour.

Vacuum Cleaner

Carpet sweepers are efficient devices to use instead of your vacuum cleaner. Try to save your vacuum cleaner for the tougher jobs.

Kitchen Disposal

When you operate your food disposal, use cold instead of hot water. The cold water saves energy and solidifies the grease which can then be ground up and washed away.

Electric Blanket

Consider using down quilts or electric blankets and turn down your heating system during the night. You will sleep comfortably and the thermostat can be set at 60°.

WATER CONSERVATION

The average homeowner pays between two hundred and three hundred dollars annually for water supply, sewage, and hot-water heating. By modifying your present plumbing fixtures, piping, and water-use habits, you should be able to reduce household water consumption substantially without loss of comfort or hygiene. If you are in need of replacement fixtures, an investment in water-efficient fixtures could save $160 per year.

In addition to saving money, there are other benefits to water conservation. All of the water used in your home becomes sewage and must be treated. If you have a backyard septic system, decreased waste loads will reduce the risks of overburdening your system, especially if it is old or undersized. If your home is plumbed into a municipal treatment system, your conservation efforts will help minimize treatment loads as well as delay construction of any larger facilities. Reduced consumption will help decrease the demand on our already endangered fresh-water supplies.

You may live in an older home where water consumption is not metered. Your annual water and sewerage bill reflects the city's estimate of your household consumption based on similar metered homes. If you think your home water conservation program is effective, you may save money by having a city-authorized meter installed.

It is surprising to learn that the average American home consumes 300 gallons of water *each* day. This figure represents the cooking, cleaning, and washing needs of a four-member household. A breakdown of the pattern of this water consumption is as follows:

Toilet	40 percent	(120 gallons)
Bathing	33 percent	(99 gallons)
Laundry	12 percent	(36 gallons)
Kitchen Sink	10 percent	(30 gallons)
Bathroom Sinks	3 percent	(9 gallons)
Utility Sink	2 percent	(6 gallons)

From these figures, it is obvious that toilets and bathing facilities offer the highest potential for water savings. (Suggestions for saving water while using your clothes washer and dishwasher are outlined in Chapter 4.) An examination of new plumbing fixtures and fittings follows.

Manufacturers names will be mentioned in reference to specific products which may not be stocked in your local plumbing supply store. A list of addresses is available on the final page of this chapter.

Toilets

A conventional water closet holds four gallons of water in its tank but uses close to six gallons per flush. This overdilution of human waste adds

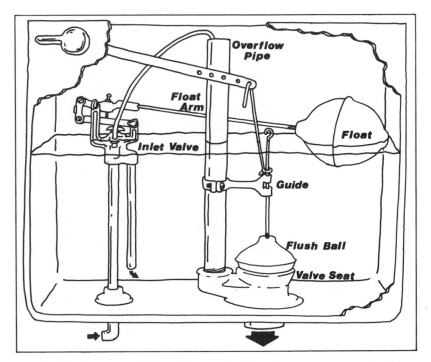

34. *The Insides of a Toilet: What to do if the toilet water is continuously running:*

1. Water Level Is Too High

a) *Bend float arm downward until water level stops ½ inch below top of overflow pipe.*

b) *Inspect inlet valve. Washers may need to be replaced. Replace whole valve if worn.*

2. Flush Ball Is Not Seating Properly

a) *Check guide and lift wire above ball. Clean or replace to get mechanism to run smoothly.*

b) *Flush ball is misaligned or deteriorated. Clean valve seat and replace flush ball.*

unnecessary strain to your septic system or municipal sewage treatment plant. With each family member requiring five uses per day, the average home flushes away approximately forty-four thousand gallons of fresh water each year. Tank modifications, new designs, and recycled wash-water systems are available, enabling you to minimize water waste without affecting the performance of your toilet.

Leaky Toilets

It is not uncommon for older toilets to leak thousands of gallons of water before being noticed. To see if water is running, lift the top off your tank and examine the flush mechanism. Often water leaks into the overflow tube because the water level is too high. This problem can be corrected by bending the float rod holding the toilet float downward to lower the water level and consequently shutting off the valve. This adjustment reduces the velocity of the flushing water and its cleansing value. Adjust the rod a minimal amount for your needs.

If you think your toilet is leaking, but you don't know for certain, add some food coloring to the water in the tank. If the coloring begins to stain the water in the bowl before the next flush, then you do have a problem. If you can not fix it yourself call in a handy neighbor or the local plumber before the problem gets worse.

The Brick Trick

Many older toilets are overdesigned hydraulically and use more water per flush than is actually required. A couple of bricks carefully placed in your toilet tank will displace some of this extra volume of water. Unfortunately, unless the bricks are made of high quality ceramic, they tend to disintegrate in the water. The decomposing particles may contribute to a malfunction of your flush mechanism. A more satisfactory solution is to place a combination of weighted plastic bottles in your tank, making sure they don't interfere with the inner workings. The containers will put much less stress than bricks on the tank and should prove effective in reducing water volume. If it is necessary to flush more than once to cleanse the bowl, you've eliminated your water-saving effect. Decrease the number of containers displacing the water to retain a margin of waste—a one-gallon reduction is generally your maximum possible savings.

Modified Toilet Tanks

Several manufacturers sell kits with prefabricated inserts designed to fit into your tank and reduce the amount of flushable water. These kits are inexpensive, easy to install, and can save you one or two gallons per flush. A telephone call to your local plumbing store should provide you with specific products.

It is possible to purchase a *dual-flush mechanism* to fit into your present toilet tank. The handle of the unit is designed to activate a partial or full flush depending on how you turn it. A flip one way activates a 3.5-gallon flush for solid wastes, and the reverse motion activates a 2.5-gallon flush for urine. Ask your plumbing supplier about dual-flush devices.

A home-built dual-flush mechanism is easily installed in your tank. Attach a heavy weight (fishing sinkers or metal washers) to the shaft just above the tank ball. By releasing the handle partway through a flush cycle, the weights will force the ball to drop, close the valve, and stop the water flow. If a full flush is desired, hold the handle down to override the partial flush.

New tanks are also available which you can install to replace your old tank. One model by Flushmate uses air compressed by the incoming water to thoroughly cleanse the toilet bowl with only 2 gallons of water. Other tank models, such as the one by Geberit, have the dual-flush feature integrated into the design.

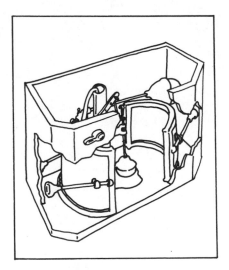

35. Tank inserts can be installed in a conventional toilet tank to reduce water used for flushing.

Shallow-Trap Toilets

Shallow-trap toilets have redesigned bowls and smaller tanks which give good flushing performance with only 3.5 gallons of water. These toilets save over 30 percent of the water normally flushed by your family.

They retail for sixty dollars and up, cost no more to install than conventional toilets, and are more compact. The major plumbing manufacturers produce shallow-trap toilets.

It is possible to purchase a shallow-trap toilet with the dual-flush mechanism. This feature, available in Geberit water-saving closets, costs more initially, but if properly used can provide a 50 percent reduction in water used for flushing. A similar model from Twyfords in England uses even less water and achieves a 70 percent water savings. A study conducted by the Federal Water Quality Administration recommended the dual cycle shallow-trap toilet as the most cost-effective water-saver available to the individual homeowner. Their studies, published in 1969, showed an annual savings of $14.45 in water costs per year for a toilet costing $145 (including installation).

Flush-Valve Toilets

You probably use a flush-valve toilet at your office. It differs from a water closet in that it uses a direct pressure valve instead of a tank to supply the water necessary for flushing. These toilets can be installed in a residence and are usually set for three gallons per flush (to conform with American sanitary standards). They require a ¾-inch copper water line instead of the usual ½-inch line and are noisy flushers. The major plumbing manufacturers sell a variety of flush-valve closets which are similar in price to conventional toilets.

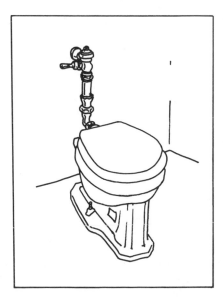

36. A direct flush-valve toilet can be set for three gallons per flush and used in the home.

Urinals

Any predominantly male household should consider the advantages of a urinal; water-saving urinals use as little as a half gallon of water per flush, resulting in a 17-gallon water savings per male per day. They cost around one hundred dollars, require a ¾-inch water supply line, and extra space in your bathroom. They are available in water-saving models from all of the major plumbing manufacturers.

Vacuum-Flush Toilets

Vacuum-flush toilets use air as the waste transport medium and require only a half gallon of water to cleanse the bowl. The disposal system includes plastic drain lines, a waste storage tank, and a vacuum pump. They are still too expensive to be considered for individual homes, but prove cost-effective for bigger applications such as multiple dwelling units. Microphor and Cycle-Let manufacture similar toilets, mostly for commerical installations.

Chemical Recirculating Toilets

These toilets, common on aircraft, repeatedly reuse the flush water after filtering, coloring, and disinfecting it. They can be installed with a holding tank or with the discharge line connected directly to the sewage system. They are expensive units to buy and install and require a costly disinfecting chemical. There is also a possibility of odor if the unit malfunctions. Aquasans is an available model which can be installed in residential bathrooms.

Incinerator Toilets

Incinerator toilets use electrical heating units to cremate the sanitary waste. They do not require any plumbing, just an electrical connection and a vent system for removing odors. Proper maintenance requires periodic removal of the ashes which are collected in a tray below the bowl. These toilets are costly to operate and are not recommended for continuous use. They can be useful in a cottage where sanitary wastes are infrequent. Incinolet and Ecolet manufacture models suitable for residential application.

Compost Toilets

A compost toilet decomposes human excrement and organic household waste in a well-aerated holding tank. It does not require any water to function, simply oxygen and time. The composting process reduces the organic material to a rich humus suitable for gardening within a six-month to two-year period. Use of a simple venting chimney eliminates any indoor odors.

Compost toilets have been a tradition in the Scandanavian countries for thirty years. They are gaining acceptance in America as the public health officials become confident of their sanitary reliability. They are expensive units to install, costing from $750 to $1,500 and are often too big for installation in an existing home. The compost toilets can handle 40 percent of the sewage load and are most practical in areas where the soil is unsuited to conventional septic systems. Write to Ecos, a distributor in Boston, for specific data on several different compost toilets.

A technical bulletin published by the University of California gives detailed plans for building an indoor composting privy for less than one hundred dollars. This privy utilizes the same design features as a commercial compost toilet but requires monthly turning of the compost.

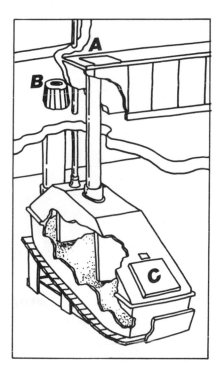

37. An aerobic composting toilet uses no water and turns organic kitchen garbage (A) and human waste (B) into humus which can be removed at hatch (C). This toilet can be considered if you are building an addition.

Recycled Water

The wash water discharged into your sewage system from the bath and laundry drains can be recycled in your home. This "gray water" is still usable for flushing your toilet which does not need potable water. There are several systems which the homeowner may adopt to recycle this water, thus saving 40 percent of normal household sewage:

A *makeshift plumbing arrangement,* usually used during periods of severe drought, is achieved by removing the trap from under the sink in your bathroom. The water drains from the sink into a large container below, to be used for toilet flushing. Keeping the plug in your tub after showers and baths will also pond adequate water for flushing. To manually flush the toilet, pour a full pail of water right into the bowl.

A more sophisticated gray water system involves *rerouting the water* from your bathtub and laundry drains into a storage tank, filtering it, and then pumping it into a pressurized tank connected to your toilet. The pressurized tank may not be necessary if the system is designed to work on a gravity feed. Again, this system will save you all of the water normally wasted by the toilet, but it involves high installation and material costs.

At first, recycled water may seem objectionable. Yet its application for flushing usually will not present any problems regarding odor or health hazards in your bathroom. The detergents from your laundry will keep the water bacteria-free. Although there are sometimes staining problems caused by metal deposits in reused water, this is easily minimized by occasional cleanings.

A recycling system can go one step further and distill the gray water for all functions except drinking and cooking. This is a complicated treatment scheme requiring bulky equipment and homeowner surveillance and maintenance. The costs of filtration, distillation, absorption, and disinfection are only reasonable for centralized recycling systems in multiple dwelling units.

Rainwater can be worth collecting especially if the rainfall in your area is high. The soft water can be stored and diverted for a variety of household tasks that do *not* require drinking water. Well-maintained rain gutters and downspouts are the collectors for a system that can be either simple or complex. A complex rainwater schematic for toilet flushing includes underground cisterns supplied by rain leaders (and city water for dry spells). The stored rainwater is pumped through a filter to a pressurized tank where it is supplied by separate piping to the toilets.

Water-Saving Fittings

Conserving water in your bathroom and kitchen can reduce your present hot-water consumption and fuel bills. These savings are possible when flow-reduction devices are installed in showers and sinks. Major reductions can be accomplished without a loss in convenience.

Low-Flow Shower Heads

The average shower takes five to ten minutes with the water running at six gallons or more per minute. The minimum 30-gallon shower can be reduced by 50 percent with shower heads that restrict the flow of water to 3 gallons of water per minute (gpm). These water-conserving shower heads are available at most hardware and plumbing stores and retail from five to thirty-five dollars. Investment in a 3-gpm head can save you twenty dollars per year for hot water costs.

If you wish to use your old shower head, you can purchase a flow control valve that fits into the water supply line and maintains an efficient flow. A *pressure sensitive* control is optimal, such as the Aquamizer by American Standard, but any similar device is a good buy for around three dollars. After installation, remember to use pipe-joint compound for a good seal.

A penny washer will also restrict the volume of water flowing through your shower head. Simply unscrew the head from the pipe that is angled at 45 degrees. Place a heavy ⅜-inch sink washer inside the female part of the shower head, then replace the head. This *restricting valve* should do the trick, at least on a temporary basis. To check your water flow rate, time the number of seconds it takes to fill a 2-gallon pail.

Low-Flow Faucets

The most successful way to reduce the usual 3-6 gpm water flow in your faucets is to use *aerator fittings*. These screenlike devices fit on the end of your taps and allow only 50 percent of the water to flow through. Aerators produce a smooth, even stream of water. They retail in supermarkets for as little as ninety-eight cents and are well worth the investment. Before buying, measure the diameters of your taps and buy male/female-threaded aerators to be sure of a proper fit. Often new faucet combinations are designed with the aerator already installed.

New faucets are available with integral *flow adjustors* for the hot and cold water supply. They deliver a dense, well-defined spray of 1 to 1.5 gallons per minute suitable for the bathroom. Since these fittings sell for about fifty dollars, low-flow faucets are most practical for a new home or as replacement hardware. They can also be used in the kitchen but should be adjusted for a 2-gpm flow. Check your plumbing store for suitable models, or investigate Unatap or Color Temp model faucets.

Pressure compensating flow-reduction devices can be installed on faucet supply lines. Note that such fittings should not be installed on a line that supplies your dishwasher because they will prevent full washing performance. These throttling devices are best installed as close to the faucets as possible to prevent any conflict with building code requirements. They are difficult to adjust and require a plumber for installation. Walker Crossweller and Control Division have an assortment of valves available for faucet-flow reduction.

Leaky Faucets

Dripping faucets can account for hundreds of gallons of wasted water per day. Obviously, any leaky faucets in your home should be repaired immediately. A pinhole leak often requires a new washer replacement which is easily installed by a handy person. Call your plumber if you need more serious repairs.

Outdoor Use

In some parts of the country, more water is used for lawn sprinkling than the combined indoor consumption. This water does not contribute to your sewage load, but the 10-gpm rate for the smallest hose size necessitates more careful water management.

To minimize water waste while sprinkling, use a sprinkling device engineered to restrict the flow of water and provide effective dispersal of the spray. A time control can save water bills when sprinklers and hoses are left unattended.

Water can also be saved when you wash your car. A hose used sparingly with a bucket of soapy water will reduce your normal water waste.

Habits—A Change for the Better

Water conservation habits require an awareness of water use combined with common sense. Here are a few basic rules for no-waste habits.

Any time you require water from the kitchen or bathroom faucets, pond just enough water for your needs. This procedure should be used for such tasks as scrubbing vegetables, rinsing dishes, brushing your teeth, and shaving.

Shower with care. The amount of time you spend in the shower, combined with the water flow rate and temperature, will determine the amount of water you use. Reduction in your hot water demand will make a noticeable difference in your fuel bill. A normal tub bath uses less than 25 gallons per use—a better bathing choice for lovers of long showers.

Use detergents and soaps wisely. Excessive sudsing requires extra rinsing for dishes and does not contribute to better cleaning in your automatic washing appliances. The phosphates in your detergents add to water pollution. Check the labels of detergents and purchase only low-phosphate cleaning products.

Flush only when necessary. Using your toilet as a garbage receptacle is a waste of water. Place an ashtray and a garbage can in your bathroom for disposal of cigarette butts, facial tissues, etc.

Manufacturers' Products and Addresses

Aquamizer
American Standard
P.O. Box 2003
New Brunswick, N.J. 08903

Aquasans
Chrysler Corp.—Space Division
P.O. Box 29200
New Orleans, La. 70129

Color Temp
Speakman Products
33-09 37th Avenue
Long Island City, N.Y. 11101

Control Division
Eaton Corp.
191 East North Avenue
Coral Stream, Ill. 60187

Cycle-Let
Thetford Corp.
P.O. Box 1285
Ann Arbor, Mich. 48106

Ecos (Composting Toilet Dist.)
21 Imrie Road
Boston, Mass. 02134

Ecolet
Recreation Ecology Conservation
9800 West Bluemound Road
Milwaukee, Wisc. 53226

Eljer Plumbingware
Wallace Murray Corp.
Three Gateway Centre
Pittsburgh, Pa. 15222

Flushmate
Water Control Products
1100 Owendale
Troy. Mich. 48084

Geberit
P.O. Box 2008
Michigan City, Ind. 46360

Incinolet
Research Products
2639 Andjon Drive
Dallas, Tex. 75220

Microphor
P.O. Box 490
Willets, Cal. 95490

Technical Bulletin No. 1
"Composting Privy"
Natural Energy Design Center
Department of Architecture
University of California
Berkeley, Calif. 94720

Twyfords Limited
P.O. Box 23
Stoke-On-Trent, Staffordshire
STA 7AL
England

Unatap
Walker Crossweller & Co., Inc.
140 Greenwood Avenue
Midland Park, N.J. 07432

RENEWABLE ENERGY SOURCES

PART 2

SOLAR ENERGY

Solar energy is not a space-age solution to the energy crisis. It is one of many tools which we, as homeowners and homebuilders, should use to reduce our dependence on fossil fuels.

☐ The technology is well known.
☐ The hardware is commercially available.
☐ The expertise for design and installation is available.
☐ The costs can be estimated from available data.
☐ Conventionally fueled auxiliary systems can supplement the solar power supply.
☐ Only a small amount of electricity is required to operate the solar pumps or fans and controls.

In recent debates among solar experts the impatient voices of the consumers repeatedly ask, "Does this have value for me? Can I use solar energy? If so, how?" This section attempts to extract the most relevant information, without the mystique of high technology, and fill the gap between the emerging solar energy industry and the interested energy consumer. The first section describes solar system applications for domestic water heating, space heating, cooling and swimming pool heating. The second section provides detailed descriptions of solar energy system components and consumer guidelines on products and operating methods.

Applications

Domestic Water Heating

It is now financially and technically feasible to heat your domestic hot water with solar energy. Solar water heaters were used in Florida and California before the availability of natural gas. Similar units are in use throughout Japan, Israel, and Australia and thousands of systems are already working in the United States. You can buy a solar water-heating package from one of many manufacturers, or purchase and assemble the components yourself. You can have the water heating system integrated with a solar space heating system.

Since water heating often accounts for 15 to 20 percent of your monthly energy bill, a simple water-heating installation can be an excellent investment. Although each home and installation is different, a conservative example will provide some guidelines:

☐ Solar installation costs: $1,500.

☐ Annual conventional fuel savings: $180 ($15 per month).

☐ Consider the solar cost as a capital investment and the fuel savings as a return on that investment.

☐ Annual return on investment: 12 percent.

☐ A home-built system will cost less and produce a greater return on investment.

☐ If you borrow the money you will probably find that your monthly financing costs are lower than the monthly fuel savings.

☐ Once the total fuel savings equals the amount of the initial investment you will be heating water for practically no cost. Operating, maintenance, and auxiliary water-heating costs are usually minimal.

In the average American household, each person uses 20 gallons of hot water per day. You can lower this demand by using the water conservation measures suggested in Chapters 4 and 5 to reduce the size and cost of the solar installation.

The water service to your home, from municipal supplies or a private well, ranges between 40°F (4.5°C) and 60°F (15.5°C) depending on the source and season. The task is simply to heat this water to about 110°F (43°C) for household needs.

The equipment for the system includes solar collectors, storage tank, pumps, controls, associated piping, insulation, and in some cases a heat exchanger and antifreeze solutions. Standard plumbing and electrical devices connect the components and regulate the operation. The required collector area and storage volume is small and most existing homes can easily accommodate the installation. If you are not eager to do it yourself, a local contractor can install the system using the manufacturer's instructions.

The *solar collector* is the most important component in determining the performance and cost of the system. Collectors absorb solar radiation, convert it to heat, and transfer the heat through pipes to storage. The following guidelines apply to most installations:

☐ Using *flat plate* type collectors to supply most of your hot water requires about 20 square feet of collector area per person.

☐ The collectors optimally should face due south, but deviations up to 20 degrees to the east or west or south are acceptable.

☐ The collectors should be mounted at an angle from the horizontal equal to the local latitude. This provides maximum exposure to the direct solar radiation throughout the year. Deviation from the optimal tilt up to 10 degrees will not materially reduce performance.

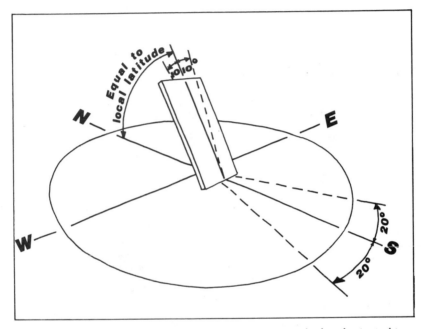

38. For domestic water heating the solar collectors are tilted and oriented to receive the maximum amount of direct solar radiation throughout the year.

Your house probably does not have a roof pitched to the south at the optimal angle. You can either increase the collector area to produce the required output or mount the collectors on a framework on the roof, walls, fence, or on the ground.

The *solar storage tank* should be sized to hold approximately one gallon for each square foot of collector area. If your existing domestic water-heating tank—either gas- or oil-fired, or electric—is in good condition, you can use it as an extra storage tank or as the auxiliary water heater.

The *circulating pump* must be adequate to circulate the water between the collectors and the storage tank.

The operation of the system is regulated by an automatic *differential controller* which responds to temperature readings from the collector and from the storage tank. When the water in storage is below the desired temperature and solar energy is available, the controller activates the system. When no solar energy is available, your backup water heater is automatically turned on.

All the pipes between the collector and the storage tank should be insulated. The storage tanks must also be wrapped with insulation. Many manufacturers sell insulating jackets for water tanks which further reduce the heat loss, even if your tank is factory insulated.

Cool Climates

If you encounter frequent or prolonged freezing conditions through-out the winter, it pays to keep the system protected with antifreeze

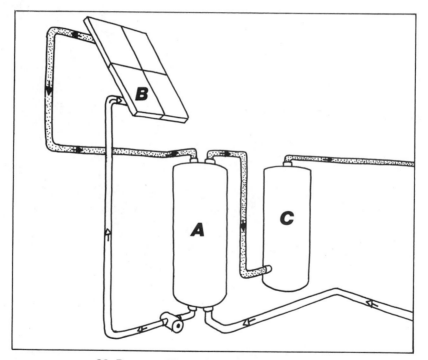

39. *Domestic Water Heating in a Cold Climate.*
*The antifreeze solution circulates in a closed loop between the collectors (A)
and the "double wall" heat exchanger (B). Cold water enters the solar storage
tank (C), circulates through the heat exchanger where it is heated. It returns to
the solar storage tank and then to the existing domestic water heater (D) for
storage or auxiliary heating.*

solution. (Antifreeze solutions are toxic and must not be allowed to mix with the potable water in the tank.) The antifreeze solution circulates through the collectors and then through a special heat exchanger which transfers the heat from the collectors to an intermediary fluid and then to the potable water. Using antifreeze and heat exchangers increases the cost of the water-heating installation and reduces its efficiency but provides reliable freeze protection.

The amount of antifreeze to use depends on your local climate. Since antifreeze reduces the heat transfer ability of water you should use the smallest amount necessary to protect the system. But be sure that it is adequate to protect against the coldest possible temperatures at your location.

Mild Climates

If you live in a mild climate where there is rarely a danger of the water freezing and bursting the pipes, the incoming water to be heated

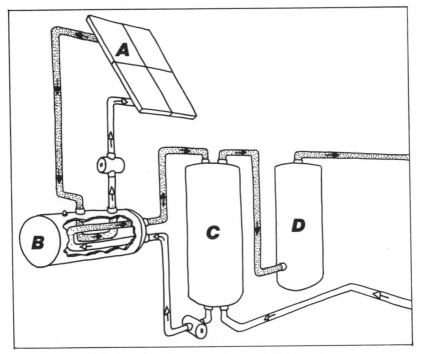

40. Domestic Water Heating in a Mild Climate.
Cold water enters the solar storage tank (A) and circulates through the
collectors (B). The solar-heated water returns to the solar storage tank and
then to the existing domestic water heater (C) for storage or auxiliary heating.

circulates through the collectors, into the storage tanks and is supplied directly to the hot-water lines. As a precaution against occasional freezing conditions, you can install a system in which the water is automatically or manually drained into the solar storage tank. Some systems automatically circulate warm water from storage through the collectors to prevent freeze-up. Or electric heat tape on the back of the collector absorber plate can be automatically activated when the outside temperature falls below 45°F (7°C).

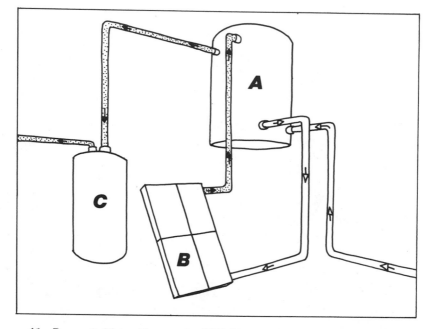

41. Domestic Water Heating in a Mild Climate Using Thermosiphoning.
Cold water enters the solar storage tank (A) and flows downs to the collectors
(B). The water being heated in the collectors rises to the solar storage tank
without the use of pumps. The heated water passes through the domestic
water-heating tank (C) for auxiliary heating, if necessary.

In mild climates you can use the natural bouyancy of heated water to operate a *thermosiphon* solar water heater. As the water is heated in the collector, it naturally rises through piping to the top of the storage tank, located above the collector. The cool water at the bottom of the tank flows down to enter the bottom of the collector. As long as the sun heats the water in the collector, the process continues without the use of a pump, automatic controls, or electricity.

If the collectors are installed on the ground or a flat roof, it is easy to place the storage tank above the collectors. In some cases the collectors are mounted on the ground outside and the tank is located inside the house.

There are many opportunities to adapt a thermosiphon system to your own specific house and site. Here are some notes of caution:

☐ The bottom of the storage tank should be at least two feet higher than the top of the collectors.

☐ The water passages in the collectors and the piping between the collectors and the storage tank should promote an open easy flow with as few joints and bends as possible.

☐ Since the system operates entirely on the energy of differential temperatures, the collectors, pipes, and tank should be heavily insulated. Losing the heat is not only wasteful but also equivalent to disconnecting the system from its energy source.

☐ The system must be protected from occasional freezing. Thermostatically activated electric heat tape on the back of the collector absorber plate is the only feasible method.

☐ Although thermosiphon systems are usually less expensive than pumped systems, they require more rigid installation locations and are rarely as efficient.

Space Heating

The major energy expense for most Americans is heating the home. (Methods of lowering the monthly heating bills are suggested in Part I.)

To install a solar heating system on an existing house (retrofitting) is an expensive project which can only be cost-effective in an energy-efficient house.

You must be able to heat your home against the coldest weather conditions even though they may occur only a few times a year. It is still too costly to buy all the solar equipment necessary to supply *all* of the heat during the coldest conditions. Most solar heating installations are carefully designed to provide 40 to 70 percent of the annual energy for a specific house and climate. Your conventionally fueled auxiliary heating system automatically provides heat when the solar system cannot satisfy the demand. In an energy independent home, a good wood-burning stove can provide the auxiliary heat. (See Chapter 7.)

You should look for the optimal economic solar investment. Over a period of years, what is the best balance between the *initial* solar system cost and the *operating* cost of your auxiliary system? This method of *life-cycle costing* considers the initial capital investment and the operating

97

and maintenance costs of heating your house over a number of years of expected use. Generalizations about the economics of solar heating are only rough guidelines. Each house must be individually analyzed to determine the optimal solution. Review the following considerations:

☐ The amount of heat your home needs depends on local weather conditions, the thermal characteristics of the house construction, your own personal comfort requirements, and habits.

☐ The cost of supplying this heat depends on which fuel you use. The availability and price of oil, gas, and electricity differ widely throughout the country and often from one town to the next.

☐ If you are considering a solar retrofit, first figure out what your actual heating bills have been and how much you can reduce them with energy conservation measures.

☐ Your decision to consider solar heating is an investment for the future. You must take into account the annual expected increase in fuel costs. Government projections for each fuel in different regions vary, but no one is predicting price reductions.

☐ The increasing conventional fuel prices are already shifting the economic balance toward higher levels of solar investment.

☐ There are many possible design variations for solar heating systems. Be sure that you are getting the right one for your home and your money.

Collectors for home heating systems require hundreds of square feet of surface area. Your home probably does not have a roof surface of adequate size with the optimal slope or orientation. The collectors can be mounted on a framework placed on the roof or on the ground adjacent to the house. The optimal collector area must be carefully calculated for each installation. It depends upon the amount of solar radiation available at your home, the efficiency of the collector type, and the percentage of solar participation desired. The following guidelines apply to most installations:

☐ The total collector area recommended is often roughly equivalent to 25 to 50 percent of the square footage of your living space to be heated. But the variables of each installation and details of accurate calculations must be examined in order to optimize the performance of the solar installations. This information is available from solar designers and government sources.

☐ The optimal collector orientation is due south to 15 degrees west of south. Deviation of more than 15 degrees will require more collector area to provide the equal amount of energy.

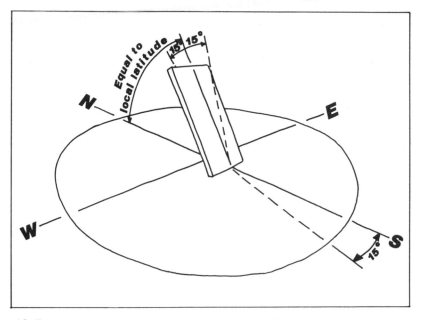

42. For space heating, the solar collectors are tilted and oriented to receive the maximum amount of direct solar radiation during the winter heating season.

☐ The optimal collector tilt is 15 degrees above the local latitude. This angled surface enables the collectors to absorb more direct radiation from the lower winter sun. Deviations of more than 15 degrees require more collector area. If your climate provides snow cover during the heating season, the collectors can be steeply tilted or even vertically installed to increase exposure to the reflectivity of the snow.

There are two types of solar space heating installations, liquid circulating systems and air-circulating systems.

Liquid Systems

A liquid solar heating installation can supply heat to your hot-water space heating system or to a forced warm-air system. It can also be used for domestic water heating and swimming pool heating. Pumps circulate water through pipes into the collectors where the water is heated and then circulated into a large solar storage tank.

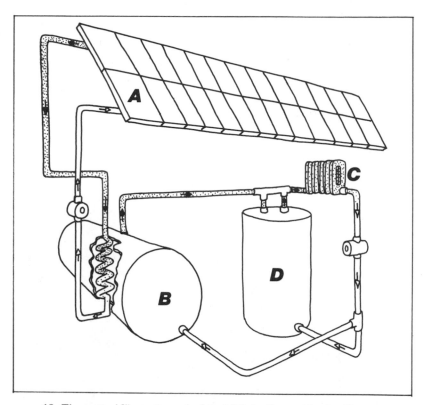

43. Theoretical Illustration of a Liquid Solar Space Heating Process.
The antifreeze solution circulates in a closed loop between the collectors (A)
and the solar storage tank (B). The heated water either circulates directly to
the heat distribution network (C) or through the existing boiler (D) for auxiliary
heating.

Advantages

1. Warm water efficiently transfers its heat to cool water or cool air. Domestic water heating, swimming pool heating and solar air conditioning (cooling) can all be included in a space heating system.
2. Less electricity is needed to operate the pumps than the fans in an air system.
3. Insulated pipes take up little space throughout the house.

Disadvantages

1. High installation costs for collectors and storage components.
2. High potential maintenance costs in the event of leaks, i.e., repairs to pipes and liquid damage done to the house.
3. Extra care and maintenance

is needed to prevent corrosion of the components.

4. System must be protected against cold weather which may freeze the water and burst the pipes, or the collector. Freeze protection usually requires antifreeze fluids or draining out the system for the colder months.

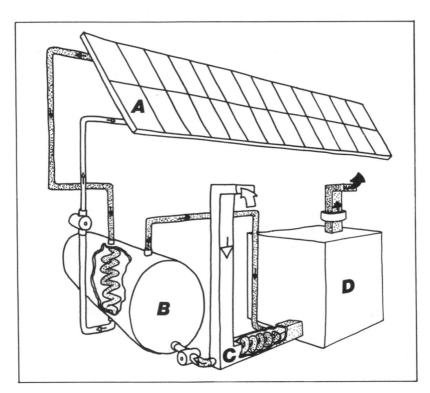

44. Theoretical Illustration of a Liquid Solar System for Heating in a Forced Warm-Air System.
The antifreeze solution circulates in a closed loop between the collectors (A) and the solar storage tank (B). The heated water circulates to the return air duct (C) and heats the air which passes through the furnace (D) for any required auxiliary heating.

The design of a liquid system must be carefully coordinated with the type of heating system you already have.

☐ If you have *hot-water radiant panels* with copper pipes imbedded inside the construction of floors, walls, or ceilings, a liquid solar system is compatible. You can be comfortably warm with radiant system temperatures as low as 85°F (29°C), which the solar system can normally provide.

☐ *Baseboard radiation units,* on the other hand, need supply temperatures of about 180°F (82°C). The flat-plate liquid collectors cannot provide this high temperature, but more advanced collectors can.

You can add new baseboard units for the solar system and rely on your existing system for backup heating.

☐ If you have a *forced warm-air* system you can also use a liquid solar system. The solar heated fluid is pumped through a heat exchange coil in the return air duct entering the furnace.

☐ A liquid solar system may also supplement your existing *heat pump* (see Chapter 3). This will extend the useful range of the solar system. Although a heat pump uses electricity efficiently, extensive use will greatly increase your monthly electric bill. So you must carefully evaluate the economic trade-offs in the design of the integrated system.

Air Systems

An air system is used primarily for supplying heat to your existing forced warm-air system. In addition, it can preheat the domestic hot-water supply. Fans move cool air through ducts from the house into the collectors where the air is heated and then circulated into the rooms or into a large rock heat storage bin.

Advantages

1. Low equipment costs for collectors, storage, and distribution components.
2. Low maintenance costs. Leaks in ducts cause little damage to home and can usually be patched with *duct tape.*
3. Simple systems can supply warm air directly to heat the home.
4. No freeze protection is needed to keep the system operating in the coldest weather conditions.
5. No corrosion problems.

Disadvantages

1. Only partial domestic water heating is possible because of the inability of warm air to transfer its heat efficiently to water.
2. Cannot be used to power solar air-conditioning (cooling) units.
3. Large insulated air ducts take up usable space throughout the home.
4. Large insulated rock storage bin requires more space than liquid storage tank.

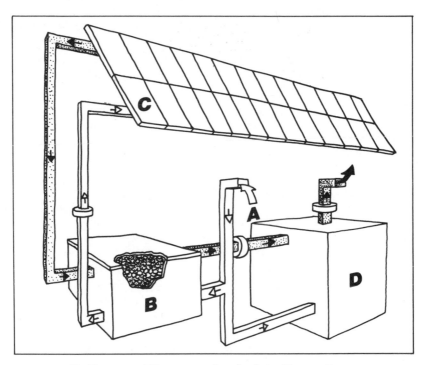

45. Theoretical Illustration of an Air Solar Heating System.
Cool air from the house (A) and the storage bin (B) circulates through the collectors (C). The solar heated air can be circulated to storage; or to the house by passing through the existing furnace (D) for auxiliary heating, if necessary.

There are usually four modes of operation. On a cold sunny day:

1. The collector-heated air is distributed into the house and the cooler return air from the house is circulated to the collectors.

2. When the house thermostat is satisfied, the collector sends the heated air into the rock storage bin charging the storage with heat and the cooler air is circulated to the collectors.

On a cold night or overcast day:

3. The heat in storage is distributed into the house and return air from the house is delivered to storage.

4. If the heat in storage is inadequate, the air circulates through the auxiliary heaters which are thermostatically controlled to boost the air temperature.

After prolonged lack of sunshine (usually three or four days) or extreme cold weather, the auxiliary heater must provide all of the heat. It must be able to accomplish 100 percent of the house's heating needs even though it will rarely be used to full capacity.

You can preheat domestic hot water with a fin coil heat exchanger inside the air duct where the solar-heated air leaves the collectors. The warm air flows over the coil, preheating the water before it returns to the conventional water-heating tank. This process requires an extra pump and heat exchanger, but has the advantage of economical operation during warm weather. The warm air can be routed to preheat the domestic water supply without heating the rock storage.

Swimming Pool Heating

The energy consumed to heat a swimming pool is a small percentage of your home's total energy usage. But several states, including New York and California, have banned the use of natural gas—the most common fuel for pool heating—for all new installations. Throughout the country there are approximately 3.5 million in-ground pools and 4 million above-ground pools with one hundred thousand new ones installed each year. A solar system will free you from rising fuel costs and increase the annual useful life of your pool. It is a relatively inexpensive and simple installation. There are about fifteen thousand solar-heated pools currently operating in the United States.

A solar system can raise the temperature of your pool by 10 to 15°. The system includes collectors, automatic controls, and piping. The pool's normal circulating pump can usually operate the solar system. There is no extra storage tank required since the pool itself stores the heated water.

The operation of the system can be quite simple. A differential controller turns on the system when the pool temperature falls below the

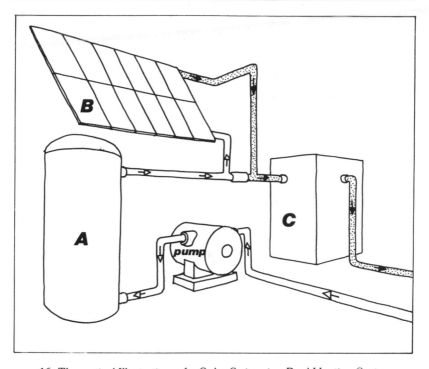

46. *Theoretical Illustration of a Solar Swimming Pool Heating System. The water is circulated from the pool through the filter (A), heated in the collectors (B), and returned to the pool through the auxiliary heating equipment (C).*

desired temperature and the sun's energy is available. The water is pumped from the pool through your pool filter, and into the collectors where it is heated and then returned to the pool. If you have a conventional pool heater, it can be automatically activated whenever necessary.

Collectors

Since swimming pools already have two of the necessary components of a solar system—a circulating pump and storage capacity—the integration of the collectors and controls into your pool system is technically simple.

You can buy *low temperature* collectors which are plastic mats or metal sheets with integral fluid passages. They are much less complex and expensive than the collectors used for domestic water heating and space heating or cooling. Consider the following guidelines:

☐ The collector area for an outdoor pool should be approximately 50 to 75 percent of the pool's surface area.

☐ The collector area for an indoor pool should be approximately 30 percent of the pool's surface area.

☐ For year-round pool heating in mild climates, the collectors should be tilted at an angle of 10 to 15 degrees lower than the local latitude. For fall and spring heating the collector tilt should be 10 to 15 degrees higher than the local latitude.

☐ If the collectors are mounted on a flat roof without a tilted framework, more collector area is required.

☐ The collectors should optimally face due south, but deviations to the west or east will not critically affect the performance.

☐ The liquid in the collectors and piping should drain down into the pool when the system is turned off.

Combined Systems

If you will be using solar energy for your domestic hot water, space heating, or cooling, then pool heating can be handled as part of the larger system. In combined solar systems the higher temperatures for the other functions require flat plate or more advanced collectors. The pool water is circulated through a heat exchanger instead of the collectors. Be sure that the heat exchanger is highly resistant to corrosion.

In combined solar systems it is important that you have adequate collector area for each use. According to your priorities, the output of the collectors can be automatically routed in response to thermostatic signals. For instance, if the system is heating the domestic hot water and the pool water, the controls will activate the pool heating loop as soon as the desired domestic water temperature is reached. Be sure that the solar controls can override the timer control on the pool filter pump so that they operate in tandem. If you want to adjust the system yourself, manual controls can easily be installed.

Reducing Heat Loss

If you reduce the amount of heat which naturally escapes from the pool, you will reduce the amount of energy required to maintain the temperature you want; this is fundamental to energy conservation. There are three ways in which your pool loses its heat:

1. *Convection.* When cool air blows across the pool surface, it picks up heat from the water. When the air is much colder than the water and the wind speed across the pool is high, these heat losses are also high.
2. *Evaporation.* The heat in the pool water is lost through vaporization at the surface.
3. *Radiation.* At night, the pool water loses its heat to the colder air.

You can reduce the convective and evaporative heat losses by lowering the air velocity at the water surface. Windscreens, such as low walls and hedges around the pool area, are effective. The radiative heat loss can be reduced with pool covers. Floating opaque plastic discs, like big lilly pads, form an effective thermal barrier and may easily be removed when the sun is shining. A transparent pool cover of thin plastic film, supported just above the water surface, will eliminate evaporative losses and reduce convection and radiation losses. Keep in mind that for outdoor pools only small amounts of heat are lost through conduction into the pool enclosure (concrete, plastic, or metal frame) and the ground around the enclosures. Therefore, extra insulation in and around the pool rarely pays off.

Solar Air Cooling

When a solar system can be utilized throughout the year for both cooling and heating, the investment is even more attractive than for heating or hot water alone.

Absorption Cooling

The most promising solar cooling method combines liquid solar heating systems with a small liquid-type absorption chiller. The average house requires only two to three tons of air conditioning.

The basic idea is similar to the old gas-fired refrigerators. The solar-heated water powers the absorption chiller. Residential-sized absorption chillers require about 195°F (90.5°C) water for maximum performance and at least 170°F (77°C) for minimal operating efficiency. Flat plate solar collectors with selective coatings and/or double glazing covers can produce these temperatures, but only for limited periods on sunny days. More advanced collectors can supply these temperatures more efficiently but are more expensive.

Depending on your local energy costs, an electric-powered refrigeration machine may be more energy efficient than a solar-fired absorption chiller with a fossil fuel auxiliary. The exception occurs in hot, arid climates where the solar system can supply 80 percent or more of the required energy for cooling.

107

Nocturnal Cooling

You can use the solar-heating system to help cool the house if you have hot, dry summers. The system can be turned on at night to radiate heat through the collectors to the cool night sky. Cooled air or water will be stored in the rock bin or storage tank. During the hot day the storage bin or tank will release cooler air and absorb the heat from the house. This method cannot be expected to satisfy the total need for air conditioning, but it can produce a measure of comfort and reduce the energy burden.

Dehumidification

The air in your house can be dehumidified by circulating it through or over a desiccant (salt material) which absorbs the moisture. When the desiccant loses its ability to absorb additional moisture, heat from the solar collectors can be used (supplementing heat from other sources) to regenerate the desiccant.

The Solar Marketplace

When you begin to shop for a solar system you will find hundreds of manufacturers each marketing his own collector as unique and superior. There are additionally hundreds of distributors, packagers, and installers of solar equipment competing for your dollars. This is an infant industry; a company with five years of commercial experience is considered an "old hand." The picture is further complicated by the fact that some of the new smaller companies produce better equipment than the older, established household names which are adding a line of solar equipment to their operations. However, some small companies have sold faulty equipment and quickly disappeared.

Buying solar is more complex than buying a household appliance. You will be making a long-term financial investment—do not be sold by advertising. Because your installation will be different in some large or small ways from any other, you should invest time to find the most effective equipment, design, and installation for your house.

When you estimate the cost of a solar system be sure to *analyze* the equipment cost. Many manufacturers quote their prices in dollars per square foot of collector. This is a problem because you want to pay for energy supplied, not for hardware. Two collectors of the same size may have different-sized absorber plates exposed to the sun. So ask for the cost per square foot of "usable collector surface." Also a complete analysis of the installation costs for your particular house is necessary. The value of the total system can only be accurately expressed as the amount of money it will initially cost to supply an approximate amount of energy each year.

Manufacturers and installers cannot provide performance guarantees on solar systems because of the variations of climate and user demand. You should, however, demand materials and workmanship guarantees. Be wary of a product with less than a five-year guarantee. Since most of these are "limited" guarantees, check to see where the manufacturer or installer's responsibility ends and yours beings. The best collector guarantees include everything except damage to the cover plates. Installation warrantees should provide for one year of free service and regular inspections.

The manufacturers' literature should include an *efficiency curve* based upon the collector's performance in testing procedures established by the National Bureau of Standards (NBSIR 74-635). If there is no such report, find out why. If the tests are done according to the manufacturer's testing procedures, ask about the NBS testing.

For detailed information on the material and equipment specifications of solar systems, refer to the "Intermediate Minimum Property Standards for Solar Heating and Domestic Hot Water Systems," available from the U. S. Department of Housing and Urban Development, Division of Energy, Building Technology and Standards, Washington, D. C. 20410.

Government Sources of Solar Information

To find out about all aspects of solar heating and cooling for homes and buildings call or write to the National Solar Heating and Cooling Information Center. The Center has been established by the U. S. Department of Housing and Urban Development (HUD) in cooperation with the Energy Research and Development Administration (ERDA) to help accelerate the widespread use of solar energy.

The Center will send you general information such as comprehensive reading lists on solar energy and summaries of residential demonstration programs. You can also request specific information about solar energy in your area: the names of architects, engineers, builders, and manufacturers doing solar work, and schedules of speakers and exhibits.

Call the Center, toll free, at (800) 523-2929 or (800) 462-4983 in Pennsylvania. You may write to the Center at Solar Heating, P. O. Box 1607, Rockville, Maryland 20850. They happily respond to thousands of requests every day.

You should also contact your state's Energy Office to find out about the latest solar legislation. Each state is considering or has passed some tax incentive legislation to encourage the use of solar energy.

Property Tax. The assessed value of your house with a solar installation may be higher than without it. A tax exemption for the increased value may be available to you.

Income Tax. A certain percentage of the cost of your solar system may be credited against personal state income tax.

Sun Rights. Some states have passed laws to safeguard your access to sunlight either by providing voluntary solar easements or by amending zoning requirements and land use planning legislation.

Sales Tax. The actual cost of solar equipment may be reduced where legislation exempts the vendors from sales tax.

Components and Installation Considerations

Solar Collector Types

The solar collectors do the same work as the boiler or furnace in your basement: they produce heat. Instead of burning oil or gas, they absorb the sun's heat directly.

Flat-Plate Collectors

The flat-plate collector is the most widely used type of collector because it can produce heat in the range of 90° to 180°F (32° to 82°C). These temperatures are suitable for domestic water heating, space heating, and, in some conditions, cooling, and for pool heating.

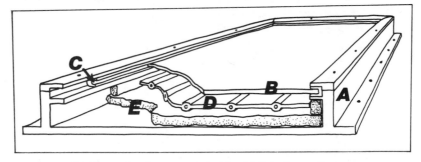

47. Example of a prototypical liquid-flat-plate collector.
(A) frame
(B) cover plate
(C) gasket
(D) absorber plate with fluid passages
(E) insulation

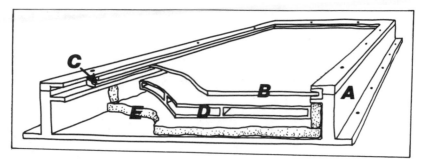

48. Example of a prototypical air-flat-plate collector.
(A) frame
(B) cover plate
(C) gasket
(D) absorber plate and air passages
(E) insulation

There are hundreds of different flat-plate collector models on the market. Since the collector is the most expensive component of a solar system, it is necessary to carefully choose the most appropriate design for your needs. Most of the collectors are similar in construction, but some of the detailed parts differ and thus affect the overall performance of the unit.

Flat-plate collectors are built as modular panels, each with a *frame* enclosing a transparent *cover plate(s), absorber plate with passages,* and *insulation.*

When sunlight falls on the collector surface, most of the solar radiation passes through the transparent cover plate, warms the absorber plate and is trapped between the cover plate and the insulation. The warm absorber plate transfers heat to the passages. The passages, in turn, warm the transfer medium (liquid or air) which flows out of the collector carrying the heat into the house.

Frames surround the collector to protect the interior parts from wind and moisture. The frames are usually metal, although fiberglass frames are used by several manufacturers. They must be light for easy handling and tightly fitted for weather protection. You should be able to open the top of the frame to service the inside parts or replace a damaged cover plate. The collector is usually bolted to the roof or supporting framework through predrilled holes along the bottom edge of the frame, called the *mounting flange.* So, look for tight weather protection (preferably nonmetallic gaskets), serviceability, and secure mounting provisions.

Cover plates are usually glass or rigid plastic sheets which allow the solar radiation to pass into the collector and then trap the heat inside.

111

They are held in place with gaskets around the top edge of the frame and sit about one inch above the absorber plate. The material of the cover plate and number of cover plates affect the performance and cost of the collectors.

Glass cover plates are usually ⅛-inch thick, although tempered glass or ¼-inch thick glass should be used for extra protection against hail or accidental damage. Glass with low iron content is best for transmitting the sunlight. Although glass is relatively stable at high temperatures, the joint at the frame must allow it to expand and contract without losing its seal.

Plastic cover plates are less expensive than glass. Many plastics are stronger, lighter, and easier to install than glass. But they usually do not trap the heat as well. Also most plastics deform after long exposure to the ultraviolet rays of the sun. They may in time turn yellow or become scratched. However, the fiberglass-reinforced polyester sheets have proven successful.

Collectors may have more than one cover plate. The advantage of multiple plates is to reduce the loss of heat from the collector to the outside air. In very cold climates two cover plates may be necessary. They are also recommended for solar air-conditioning installations which collect heat at high temperatures. A plastic sheet may be used as the inside plate where it will reduce the heat loss without being exposed to weather damage. Multiple cover plates should be separated by ½ to 1-inch of air space.

Absorber plates and passages for liquid collectors. The function of the absorber plate is to absorb the incoming solar radiation and transfer the heat to the liquid in the passages. The absorber plates are usually metal sheets (copper, aluminum, or steel) with blackened surfaces which increase the heat absorption. Flat black paint or the more expensive *selective surfaces* are most common. The criteria for the absorber material are its ability to conduct the heat and to resist corrosion.

There are three common ways of passing the liquid transfer medium through the absorber plates:

1. The Thomason method simply allows the liquid to flow down the collector over a corrugated absorber plate. This *trickle-type* collector is relatively inexpensive and has proven successful.

2. A second method allows the liquid to flow in between two metal sheets. Be sure that the metal is highly resistant to corrosion—again, copper is preferred.

3. Some absorber plates have metal tubes bonded to the plate. Many collectors have different patterns of tubing, horizontal, vertical or serpentine.

Absorber plates and passages for air collectors. The absorber plate may be made of less expensive materials than those required for a liquid system. As long as it is black on the surface, it will absorb heat from the sun and transfer it to the air blowing across it. Most manufacturers use metal plates for higher conductivity and for ease in applying the black surface coating. It is most effective to pass the air behind the absorber plate— between it and the insulation.

Insulation. It is essential that the flat-plate collector be insulated inside the frame, on the back and around the edges. Without adequate insulation, the heat absorbed by the plate will escape through the frame. In liquid collectors, the insulation should be separated from the absorber plate by about one inch. In air collectors, the insulation should be about one to three inches from the absorber plate.

The best way to evaluate the insulation is not by the thickness but by its actual ability to resist heat flow. This capability is listed as an R value. An R value of 11 should be the minimum on the back while a slightly lower rating is acceptable along the edges. If the collector is mounted on a vertical wall, less insulation is required. Collectors mounted away from the house or on a separate framework exposed to wind need more than the R-11 rating.

Fiberglass and mineral wool are recommended insulation materials because they can withstand high temperatures without deterioration. In fact, all internal collector components should be able to withstand temperatures up to 400°F (204°C). This guideline will protect you from any material which might decompose, give off toxic gases, or burst into flames under extremely high operating temperatures.

Swimming Pool Collectors

These panels are built to heat the water in a swimming pool by 10 to 15°F—enough to add months of use to your pool.

Most low-temperature collectors are only slightly more sophisticated than a black garden hose exposed to the sun. They are usually blackened plastic mats or metal sheets with fluid passages built into the panels. Most panels are made without frames, insulation, or cover plates so they are much less expensive than flat-plate collectors.

Even for this relatively simple type of collector, there are several important criteria for you to check:

☐ Plastic collectors must be resistant to the damage which may be caused by the sun's ultraviolet rays.

☐ The fluid passages in plastic collectors must be resistant to algae, minerals, and pool chemicals. In metal collectors the passages are usually copper tubes for the same reason.

113

☐ Since there is no frame, the mounting procedure requires special attention. Some roofs are uneven (wood shingles, clay tiles) and some are rough (pebbles on a built-up roof). Be sure that the panels are installed to lie smooth—sometimes a pad or underlayment is necessary to keep the panels rigid.

High-Temperature Collectors

These collectors can produce the required temperatures for solar air conditioning as well as space and water heating. But because of their current technical complexity and high cost it will probably be several years before homeowners are using them.

While the flat-plate units absorb solar energy on a large absorber plate, high temperature collectors *reflect* the sunlight and *focus* it onto a small absorber surface. They must continuously face the direct sunlight in order to keep the absorber in focus. The collector must follow the sun. Automatic or manually operated movable collector mounts are built into the collector unit.

High-temperature collectors use fluid transfer mediums. In a *linear*-concentrating collector, the reflectors focus radiation along the tube-absorber which is carrying the fluid. In a *circular*-concentrating collector the reflectors, shaped like a cone, focus the radiation on one point. There the fluid, passing through the small absorber, picks up the heat.

When these units become cost-effective investments, be sure to consider these issues:

☐ The heat-producing ability of the collector should match your needs. It doesn't make sense to buy an oven to toast your bread.

☐ These collectors do not function at all on cloudy or overcast days Make sure that your climate is suitable.

☐ The reflective surfaces must be of proven durability and have easy access for cleaning.

☐ The tracking mechanisms must be accurate, durable, and simple to maintain. If it fails, the system doesn't just lose efficiency—it is a total loss.

There are several high-temperature collectors which combine the absorbing characteristics of flat-plate type and the reflecting capacity of the concentrating type. Some *tubular* and *evacuated tube* collectors are efficient at high temperatures.

Solar Collector Mounting

Collectors should be mounted where they can receive at least six hours of direct sunlight each day. Be certain that they are not shaded by

114

nearby buildings or trees. Even parts of your own home, such as high roofs, chimneys, and walls, may cast shadows on the collector area. In urban areas, the issue of "sun-rights" (i.e., a proposed building which would obstruct your access to sunlight) is now a legal problem of zoning regulations.

Fixed mounting is normally most appropriate for a home since it requires little maintenance. The fixed collectors must be set to the optimal tilt and orientation for the location and use intended. Collector output can be increased by placing a reflective surface such as Mylar-faced plywood in front of fixed mounted units. These surfaces may be adjustable to increase the reflectivity at different times during the year or to cover the collectors when not in use.

The majority of collectors are sold as *surface-mounted* units. They can be installed on any suitable surface (i.e., roof, framework, etc.).

With liquid collectors mounted on a roof, an extra waterproof membrane should be installed under the collectors to prevent water damage to the interior of the house in case of leaks. The collectors should be raised slightly above the roof surface to allow rainwater to pass underneath the collector frame.

Sloping Roofs

In existing homes it is very unusual to find optimal mounting conditions—especially for solar heating or cooling which require large collector surfaces. You can set the collectors on a framework on the sloping roof although this is often a large extra expense. Remember that the collectors should be located for easy access—a difficult consideration on sloped roofs.

49. Solar collectors mounted on a sloping shingled roof.
(Courtesy: Northeastern Solar Energy Corp.)

Flat Roofs

An existing home with a flat roof may provide an excellent opportunity for a solar installation. Surface-mounted collectors can be placed on a tilted framework. If there is easy access to the roof you may take advantage of a movable mount to increase the collector output or use reflective panels in front of the collectors. When the collectors are installed in parallel rows (sawtoothed configuration) you can cover the back (north-facing) side of the framework with reflective material (such as Mylar-coated plywood) to increase the sunlight on the collectors behind it.

50. Solar collectors mounted on a frame above a flat roof.
(Courtesy: Daystar Solar Inc.)

Here are several hazards with flat-roof installations:

☐ Snow buildup can block the collector surface. Keep the bottom of the units 18 inches above the roof.

☐ Wind can push behind an open mounting framework and damage or dislodge the collectors. Close off the north face of the framework.

☐ Be careful that one row of collectors does not shade the row behind it—especially in winter when the shadows are longest.

☐ When the collectors are mounted on a framework, the weight distribution on the roof may be uneven. Careful structural planning is required before the installation.

116

Vertical Walls

Collectors on the south wall are useful for homes located above 42 degrees latitude where space heating is the primary concern. Reflected sunlight from snow cover or white gravel will increase the collector output.

Be aware of the following:

☐ They will not adequately heat domestic water the year round because of the minimal sunlight striking the vertical surface during the spring, summer, and fall.

☐ The danger of snow buildup and mud accumulation suggests raising the bottom of the collector several feet above the ground.

Ground Mounting

If you have flat- or south-facing land near the house, the collectors may be installed on a framework. This method provides easy access for maintenance. It also eliminates the need for any structural, mechanical, or aesthetic alterations to the roof. Ground mounting makes good sense for multiple dwelling developments. A large central collector area can serve all the houses and eliminate the architectural restraints imposed by

51. Ground-mounted solar collectors on a frame adjacent to the house. (Courtesy: Northeastern Solar Energy Corp.)

optimal collector requirements on each house. Obviously, any such common or shared facility requires cooperation among the occupants.

Some warnings about these ground mounted installations:

☐ The possibility of the collectors being shaded by nearby terrain, foliage, or man-made objects is greater than for collectors mounted on the house.

☐ Snow buildup and mud accumulation require raising the collectors several feet above the ground.

☐ Accidental damage or vandalism is more likely and the collector area may have to be fenced in.

☐ Be sure that the pipes or ducts from the collector to the storage area in the house are well insulated. Otherwise the collected heat will dissipate along the route.

Heat Storage

The storage of heat, which was necessary in pre-industrial times, is essential in solar energy systems. Sunlight is the fuel we cannot store, so we store the heat captured from the sun. In most climates, our homes often require heat when the sun is not shining on it—at night and on heavily overcast days. When the sunlight is available, it is necessary that the collectors be able to capture more heat than the house demands and to keep the excess in storage for space heating and domestic water heating. For swimming-pool heating, the water in the pool serves as its own storage facility.

Air Systems

Air systems usually store heat in rocks which are contained in a bin connected by ducts to the collectors. When the house is warm enough and sunlight is still available you can begin to "charge" the storage—to store heat.

Size of Rock Bin. The storage volume should be sized in relation to the collector area. As a guideline you should have about ¾ of a cubic foot of rock bed for each square foot of collector area.

Location. For existing houses the most practical solution is to build the bin underground near your house. It should be placed below the frost line to protect it from movement and it should also be above the water table and away from septic tanks.

Insulation. The storage bin must be well insulated to prevent the heat from escaping. Proper insulation should have a value of R-19, about six inches of fiberglass or its equivalent. If the bin is within a living space, insulation is also needed for control of the heat.

The Rocks. It is important that the rocks be the right size and shape. The hot air must be able to flow around them. Rounded river rock about 2 inches in diameter will provide the proper surface area and open space between them. Sharp-edged rocks will wedge together and prevent the adequate flow rate of the air. If the rocks are too large there will be less surface area and therefore inadequate heat retention. Be careful that the rock is thoroughly washed before installation so that dirt is not picked up by the heated air and blown into the living spaces.

Preheating Domestic Hot Water. Significant energy savings can be made by reducing the burden on the conventional water heater. The incoming cold water can be heated as it passes through a copper pipe or a small tank imbedded in the rock storage bin. The preheated water then flows into the conventional water heating tank. When pipe is used, a long run inside the rock bin will increase the heat transfer so serpentine configurations are often installed. A problem occurs if there is a leak in the imbedded pipe or tank. Be sure that every precaution to prevent leaks is taken—the quality of the pipe and careful installation are essential considerations.

Salts for Heat Storage. A major breakthrough in heat storage for solar air systems will occur when phase-changing salts become technically and economically viable.

Phase-changing salts have a low melting point ranging from 84° (29°C) to 120°F (49°C) which, when heated to that temperature, change from solid crystals to liquid and absorb (store) heat. When the temperature falls, the liquid changes back to solid crystals and the stored heat is released. In this way, a large amount of heat can be stored and released by a small volume of material.

The main problem with salts, in addition to their high cost, is that they lose their phase-changing ability after repeated cycles. Hopefully, the problems will soon be solved and this method will become commercially available.

Liquid Systems

In liquid solar systems the heat is stored in water. If you are using solar for domestic hot water only, the heated water is stored in the solar storage tank and in your existing domestic water heating tank. Liquid systems for home heating require much larger storage tanks.

Size of Liquid Storage Tank. The size of the storage tank must be designed along with the collectors and the heat distribution system. It often works out to be roughly two gallons of storage for each square foot

119

of collector, or the number of gallons of storage equals the number of square feet of heated space in the house.

Location. The tank should be located near the boiler or furnace and domestic water heater if possible. Be sure that there is open space around the tank for easy access to the fittings. If there is a heat exchanger in the tank you must leave room for inserting and removing it. Wherever the tank is placed, extra structural support is necessary. The tanks are often buried in the ground near the house. If you have a large insulated basement or crawl space, you may be able to build the tank inside the house by assembling the parts which can fit through existing passages.

Types of Tanks:

Concrete with Waterproof Plastic Lining. If you are building a sizable addition to your house a concrete tank may be built-in with the foundation. This is less expensive than buying and installing a freestanding tank. It eliminates the problem of corrosion associated with metal tanks. The quality of the impermeable liner is critical because if a leak does develop it will be difficult to trace in the concrete.

Fiberglass. Because a fiberglass tank comes as one large unit and has to fit through large openings, it is rarely used as indoor storage in existing homes. Corrosion and leakage are eliminated but fiberglass tanks should not be used to store water above 160°F (71°C).

Glass-Lined Steel. They are superior to the galvanized steel tanks which often have problems with corrosion and leakage.

Galvanized Steel. If you buy the less expensive galvanized steel unit you should add chemical corrosion inhibiters to protect the tank. Since these chemicals are usually considered toxic, do not run the domestic water heating pipes or heat exchangers through the tank.

Insulation. All water storage tanks should be insulated. Depending on the construction of the tank you can use vermiculite, mineral wool, or fiberglass. Sprayed polyurethane foam is often used in tanks buried underground. It is an excellent insulator but gives off toxic fumes if it burns. The minimum insulation value to look for is R-19.

Controls

In your conventional heating system, the house thermostat senses the indoor temperature. When it falls below a set number—the minimum comfortable temperature—the thermostat electrically calls for heat. It doesn't matter whether the sun is shining or if it is day or night. The source of the energy is already there—gas, oil, or electricity.

A solar system depends on the outside weather conditions for its source

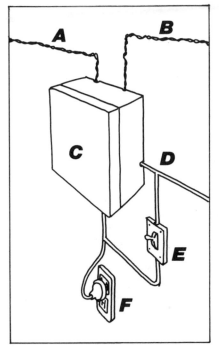

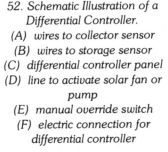

52. *Schematic Illustration of a Differential Controller.*
(A) *wires to collector sensor*
(B) *wires to storage sensor*
(C) *differential controller panel*
(D) *line to activate solar fan or pump*
(E) *manual override switch*
(F) *electric connection for differential controller*

of energy. A control mechanism is needed to collect and store this heat. The controls generally work like this:

1. The temperature at the collector is measured by an automatic sensor.
2. The temperature in the storage bin or tank is measured by an automatic sensor.
3. These sensors are connected to a *differential controller,* a small electrical device which compares the temperature readings from the sensors.
4. The solar system pumps or fans are turned on and off automatically by signals from the differential controller.
5. You can override the controller with manual switches.

Controls can become overcomplicated, especially when the solar system is designed to supply heat for more than one purpose. A large solar installation can be used for space heating, domestic water heating, and pool heating; and the heat from the collectors can be automatically routed in response to electrical signals for each function. Guidelines to solar control networks include the following:

Overdesign. There is a common tendency to overdesign control systems. Be aware that the basic functions must indeed be regulated, but you are not guiding a lunar landing module. In fact, each extra control has a potential for mechanical malfunction. So keep the circuitry as simple as functionally possible.

Indicator Panel. If the system is serving serveral functions, be sure to install an *indicator panel.* It is a simple box with little lights which tell you what the system is doing. Is it heating the storage, the pool, or the domestic water? Is it on or off? If you like to play with this sort of thing, you can put switches next to each indicator and manually change the operation. This manual override is especially helpful during the spring and fall when heating demands are shifting. It enables you to control the use of the energy which is being generated at home.

Thermometers. It is helpful to have thermometers you can read at critical points along the solar circuit. You can read the temperatures at the following points: (a) collector inlet; (b) collector outlet; (c) top of the storage tank or rock bin; (d) bottom of the storage tank or rock bin; (e) heat exchanger inlet; (f) heat exchanger outlet.

You can roughly check that the system is doing its job when (a) is lower than (b) by 5 to 20°, (c) is higher than (d), and (e) is higher than (f) by 5 to 10°.

Location. The exact location of the automatic temperature sensors is important. In a *liquid collector* the sensor should be inside the pipe which leads the warmed liquid away from the collector. In an *air collector* the sensor should be on the air stream side of the absorber plate over which the heated air is passing—usually the bottom side, facing the insulation. This will insure that the sensor is reading the actual heat-collecting ability, not the possible heating potential near the collector. For *low temperature plastic-type pool heating collectors,* the sensor can be placed next to the panel.

The location of the sensor in the storage depends on the type of storage unit. Be sure that it is placed so that it is reading neither the highest nor the lowest temperature being stored. You should also request a high-temperature cutoff device inside the solar water storage tank to automatically turn off the system when the storage temperature reaches about 180°F (82°C). This device is often required by local plumbing codes to prevent overheating.

Differential Controller. The differential controller should be set to turn the system on when the collector sensor is at least 10° above the storage sensor, and turn it off when the differential is 3°.

If it is set at a lower differential, the pump or fan will often *overcycle,* that is, it will turn on and off too many times when the collector and storage temperatures are almost equal.

If it is set too high—for instance, above a 20° differential—you will miss out on collecting a lot of heat.

Automatic Controls. The conventional backup heater must operate in tandem with the solar-heating system. When the storage temperature falls below the desired setting and there is no solar energy to collect, the auxiliary heater must automatically turn on.

For home heating, the auxiliary boiler or furnace should be used to supply *only* the heat demanded by the house thermostat. It should not be used to heat the solar storage water tank or rock bin.

For domestic water heating, however, the auxiliary heater should automatically heat the storage if there is only one tank. Where there are two tanks, the auxiliary heaters should heat only the second one in the series, the other one being used for storage.

Further Reading

1. Farrington Daniels, *Direct Use of the Sun's Energy,* New Haven, Conn., Yale University Press, 1964.

Comprehensive descriptions of solar energy theory and applications.

2. *Solar Dwelling Design Concepts.* Available from the U. S. Department of Housing and Urban Development.

3. Steve Baer, *Sunspots,* Alburquerque, New Mexico, Zomeworks Corporation, 1975.

7

WOOD POWER

If you have a nearby source of wood you should consider wood heating for your home. Depending on local fuel prices, wood heat may be cheaper than the oil, natural gas, or electric heat you are presently buying. You can use wood either as your auxiliary or primary heat source in the following ways:

☐ If you have a working masonry chimney, you can modify your fireplace to improve its efficiency and supply auxiliary heating.

☐ You can close off the fireplace opening and connect a wood-burning stove to the chimney for room heating.

☐ If you have forced-air heating, you can add a wood-burning furnace to the system as the primary or auxiliary heat source.

☐ You can install a wood-burning stove with a prefabricated metal chimney for room heating.

☐ Wood-burning equipment can be integrated with a solar-heating system, either as the primary or auxiliary heat source.

Annual Wood Consumption

It is helpful to know how much wood you will need before the heating season starts. Generally speaking, a good wood-burning furnace can provide adequate heat in a well-insulated three-bedroom home with four cords of air-dried, high-density hardwood. Consult Chart 7 for a list of high-, medium- and low-density tree species. If you burn wood of medium density, multiply the above figure by one and one-half. A low-density wood will double the four-cord figure.

If you intend to use a wood stove to heat part of your home, your fuel needs will be substantially decreased. It is best to buy or cut more wood than you think you will need. You can burn the excess in next heating season.

Some background on wood will help you decide whether it is the fuel suited to your heating needs.

Wood as Fuel

Wood is a renewable resource if the harvested timberlands are properly managed. It is a relatively clean fuel, burning cleaner than oil and coal. Wood heat requires more work and personal attention than a conventional heating system. Even an efficient stove needs two daily stokings and ash removal twice a month.

All oven-dry wood has basically the same energy potential, pound for pound. It is the density of the wood that makes the biggest difference— the denser the wood the greater the heat value and the better it is for fuel. Resin content also increases a wood's energy potential, but it adds to sparking and smoking problems.

You should know which woods are easier to ignite, easier to split, and their general ratings as fuel. These characteristics are outlined in Chart 8.

—————————————Chart 7—————————————

*Densities of Various North American Woods**

HARDWOODS

High	Medium	Low
Live oaks	Sugar maple	Red alder
Eucalyptus	American beech	Large tooth aspen
Hop hornbeam	Honey locust	Basswood
Dogwood	Yellow birch	Chestnut
Hickory	White ash	Catalpa
Shadbush	Elm	Black willow
Persimmon	Black gum	Box elder
White oak	Red maple	Tulip poplar
Black birch	Black walnut	Butternut
Black locust	Paper birch	Quaking aspen
Apple	Red gum	Cottonwood
Blue beech	Cherry	Willow
Crabs	Holly	Balsam poplar
Red oak	Gray birch	
	Sycamore	
	Oregon ash	
	Sassafras	
	Magnolia	

SOFTWOODS

High	Medium	Low
Slash pine	Yew	Ponderosa pine
Pond pine	Tamarack	Red fir
Western larch	Nut pines (pinyon)	Noble fir
Longleaf pine	Shortleaf pine	Black spruce
	Junipers	Bald cypress
	Loblolly pine	Redwood
	Douglas fir	Hemlocks
	Pitch pine	Sitka spruce
	Red cedar	Yellow cedar
	Norway pine	White spruce
		White pine
		Balsam fir
		Western red cedar
		Sugar pine

*From *The Complete Book of Heating with Wood,* by Larry Gay, p. 36.

Supply From Woodlot

If you own wooded property, each acre should provide you with one-half to one cord of usable firewood per year. It isn't always necessary to cut down trees; pruning and picking up broken limbs will yield a good harvest.

Slow and modest thinning of the straightest, densest tree species will increase the value of your woodlot. Woodlot owners should consult their state's Department of Environmental Conservation for free advice. In many cases, a forester will formulate a management plan for your woodlot and mark the trees for cutting.

Free Wood Available

There are many opportunities for obtaining free firewood. Often woodlot owners welcome conscientious woodcutters who will remove dead or fallen trees and perform selective cutting, in return for wood collected. Utility companies, road construction projects, local dumps, and sawmills are good sources of wood, ranging from felled trees to mill scraps. Some state forests also offer wood for a small fee to private parties willing to cut and haul the marked trees.

If you live in an area where the elms have been stricken with Dutch elm disease, you can use this wood as fuel. Burn all of the infected wood before spring, or more beetles will emerge. Strip and burn the bark of any leftover wood to destroy any eggs or larvae still living in the wood.

Chart 8

*Ratings for Firewood**

Name of Trees	Easy to Burn	Easy to Split	Does it have heavy smoke?	Does it pop or throw sparks?	General Rating and Remarks
HARDWOODS					
ash, red oak, white oak, beech, birch, hickory, hard maple, pecan, dogwood	yes	yes	no	no	excellent
soft maple, cherry, walnut	yes	yes	no	no	good
elm, sycamore, gum	medium	no	medium	no	fair; contains too much water when green
aspen, basswood, cottonwood	yes	yes	medium	no	fair; but good for kindling
chestnut, yellow popular	yes	yes	medium	yes	poor
SOFTWOODS					
southern yellow pine, douglas fir	yes	yes	yes	no	good but smoky
cypress, redwood	medium	yes	medium	no	fair
white cedar, western red cedar, eastern red cedar	yes	yes	medium	yes	good; excellent for kindling
eastern white pine, western white pine, sugar pine, ponderosa pine, true firs	medium	yes	medium	no	fair; good kindling
tamarack, larch	yes	yes	medium	yes	fair
spruce	yes	yes	medium	yes	poor

*SOURCE: U.S. Forest Products Laboratory.

Purchasing Firewood

The standard measure for firewood is a *cord*. This is a volume measurement describing a stack of wood 8 feet long by 4 feet wide by 4 feet high. Although a cord should yield 128 cubic feet of wood, this is never the case. The amount of wood can vary from 60 to 100 cubic feet depending on the taper and crookedness of the wood, as well as the skill of the piler. If you do purchase by the cord, request a mixture of dense species of random sizes to guarantee a good buy.

Often a wood dealer will offer firewood by the *face cord*. A face cord is a 4-by-8-foot stack by the length of the logs. The logs can be any length, depending on the cut. Investigate the local terminology to make sure that you're getting what you're paying for. Also, the price may or may not include delivery and stacking. If a dealer is offering wood by weight, check that it is *well seasoned* or you will be paying for the moisture content. (A full cord of air-dried hardwood should weigh about two tons.) If he is selling by volume, try to buy the densest wood possible. You usually don't know whether you have bought a full cord until you have stacked it yourself.

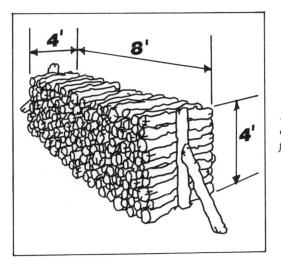

53. *A standard cord of wood measures 8 feet x 4 feet x 4 feet.*

Determining Dryness

It is important to determine whether the wood you purchase is dry. It should not look freshly cut—the ends should be cracked and dried out. If you hit two logs together listen for a ring and not a dull thud.

Storage of Firewood

Wood that is freshly cut from a live tree is "green" and needs to be "seasoned" or dried to reach its full burning potential. For immediate drying, stack the green wood in separate piles raised above the ground in a space exposed to sunlight and wind. The smaller the wood pieces and the more room between the piled rows, the faster the drying time. Also, piling the split wood in crisscross fashion will promote maximum air flow. Most wood is considered seasoned after six months, although it takes about two years to attain maximum dryness.

In wet seasons, overhead rain protection should be provided. In dryer seasons the stacks should be left uncovered in the sun. Any wood pile covered with a plastic sheet will tend to hold moisture since there is no opportunity for air circulation.

If you have a heated garage or basement, you can season your wood indoors. The warm, unhumidified air is ideal for drying wood quickly. Prior to prolonged storage, consult the U.S. Department of Agriculture for methods of preventing bug problems.

Wood will decay if stored too long, thereby decreasing its potential energy content. To prevent decay, keep the wood dry especially during the humid summer months.

Since firewood often attracts worms and insects, no more than a day's worth of wood should be stored in your living space. Bark removal will help debug your wood supply.

Green Wood

Green wood is approximately 50 percent water and 50 percent wood. It is difficult to ignite, smokey while burning, and supplies only one-fifth the heat output of a similar amount of air-dried wood. If you must burn green wood, choose the drier heartwood over sapwood, and hardwood over softwood.

Mixing green wood with your seasoned fuel wood will lengthen burning time, an advantage when stoking a cookstove or banking an overnight fire. Trial and error will teach you the most successful ratios for your stove and wood.

Splitting Wood

Splitting logs into smaller pieces will decrease drying time and promote more complete combustion when burning. Your task is made easier when you have the right tools at hand. A quality ax with an extra

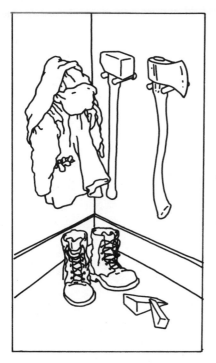

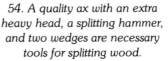

54. A quality ax with an extra heavy head, a splitting hammer, and two wedges are necessary tools for splitting wood.

heavy head plus a splitting hammer and at least two wedges are necessary for the job. Choose short lengths of unseasoned straight-grained for splitting ease.

Creosote

Creosote is the product of incomplete combustion. It is a flammable substance, made up of the unburned volatiles, which condenses on the interior of your wood-burning apparatus. To minimize creosote buildup, you must keep your chimney hot. This will discourage condensation of the gases and maintain the necessary draft. Seasoned wood burned in an airtight stove with a flue damper reduces creosote problems.

The Chimney

If your home is equpped with a masonry chimney, examine it carefully before building a fire. You need an unobstructed flue to remove the smoke and create a good draft. If your chimney is lined with hollow clay tiles, it will help maintain the necessary high temperatures. If your

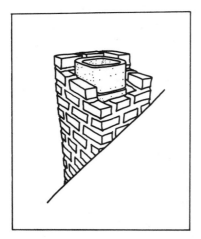

*55. A masonry chimney should be
lined with hollow clay tile.*

chimney is excessively large, you can control the draft by adding a chimney cone or by installing a damper or metal chimney piping inside the existing chimney. The chimney must be higher than the roof of your house. If your existing chimney is not high enough, you must add to it in accordance with your local building department standards.

If your home does not have a chimney, you can install an approved prefabricated metal chimney. Whether you route the chimney through the middle of your home or outside along an exterior wall, keep it as straight and vertical as possible. When purchasing stainless-steel chimney sections, check to see that the piping is recommended for the high

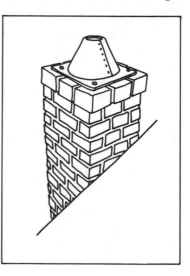

*56. Install a chimney cone to
reduce downdraft problems with
an oversized chimney.*

temperatures of a wood fire. Look for a high insulation rating and stainless steel that will be resistant to the corrosive chimney deposits. A good quality, properly installed prefab chimney should give twenty years of service.

Single-wall, uninsulated stovepipe sections are *not adequate* for a chimney. The piping will decay in an extremely short period of time. It will not meet building safety standards and will probably jeopardize your household fire insurance policy.

The diameter of your chimney will also affect performance. It must be large enough for the gases to flow but not so large that it cools off and causes smoking in your house. The chimney should always be *at least* the same diameter as the collar on your equipment. A small increase in diameter will increase capacity and may sometimes improve the overall performance of your venting system.

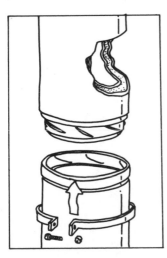

57. Prefabricated metal chimney sections must be made of high quality stainless steel and insulation. Securely clamp the sections together. This quality prefabricated metal chimney costs approximately twenty dollars per linear foot.

Smoking Problems

If your chimney smokes, you should first check your flue damper to see that it is not shut. Also check the system for obstructions and clean it if necessary.

Do not use more than one appliance per flue. If you must connect more than one stove to a single chimney, have them enter separate flues within the chimney.

The fire may tend to smoke when first lit because of a cold chimney or low air pressure inside the house. To establish a proper draft, open only the lowest windows in the room while you begin the fire, or place a piece of burning newspaper in the chimney to warm it.

Twenty causes
of chimney troubles and their cures.

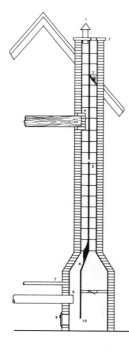

No.	Fault	Examination	Correction
1.	Pipe extension not of same area as chimney opening, and extension below opening of cap.	This is ascertained by measurement.	Pipe to be extended and opening to be same as chimney opening.
	Chimney below gable of roof.	Determined by actual observation.	Extend chimney above gable of roof.
2.	Chimney opening smaller than inside dimension.	Ascertained by measurement.	Widen opening to same dimension as chimney area.
3.	Obstructions in chimney.	Found by lowering weight on a line.	Use weight to break and dislodge.
4.	Projection into the chimney.	Lower a weight or light on extension cord.	Must be handled by brick contractor.
5.	Break in Chimney linings.	Build smudge fire blocking off other chimney opening, watching for smoke escape.	Must be handled by competent brick contractor.
6.	Collection of soot at narrow space in the opening.	Lower light on long extension cord.	Clean out with weighted brush or bag of loose gravel on end of line.
7.	Two or more openings into same chimney.	This is found by inspection from basement.	The least important opening must be closed, using some other chimney flue.
8.	Smoke pipe projects into flue but beyond surface of the wall.	Measurement of the pipe from within or observation of pipe by means of lowered light.	Length of pipe must be reduced to allow end of pipe to be flush with wall.
9.	Air leak at base of clean-out door.	Build small fire, watching for smoke or flame through the cracks.	Cement up all cracks around the base.
10.	Failure to extend the length of flue partition down to floor level.	This is found by inspection.	Extend partition to floor level.
11.	Broken clay tiles.	Can be found by light and mirror reflecting condition of walls.	All breaks should be patched with cement.
12.	Clay lining fails to come below opening of smoke pipe.	Found by observation through flue opening into chimney.	Clay tiling should be extended below flue opening.
13.	Partial projection of smoke pipe into flue area.	Found by measurement after pipe is withdrawn or by sight from chimney opening, using light on a cord.	Projection must be eliminated.
14.	Loose seated pipe in flue opening.	Air leaks can be determined by smoke test or examination of chimney while fire burns below location.	Leaks should be eliminated by cementing all pipe openings.
15.	Smoke pipe enters chimney in declining position.	This is observed by measurement.	Correct the pipe to permit smoke to enter in an as-, cending pipe.
16.	Second flue opening below that for smoke pipe.	This is found by observation from within basement.	Change to allow only one opening in each chimney.
17.	Accumulation of soot narrows cross sectional area of pipe.	Examine pipe from clean-out opening.	Remove soot.
18.	Hand damper in a full closed position.	If handle does not give true position of plate remove section of pipe to ascertain position.	Allow sufficient opening of plate for needed escape of gases.
19.	Clean-out opening on pipe leaks air.	Flames visible when furnace is under fire.	Tighten or cement to eliminate leak.
20.	Clean-out pan not tightly seated in base of chimney.	This air leak can be determined by watching action of small fire built in bottom of chimney shaft.	Cement to eliminate all leaks.

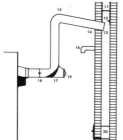

Compliments of

WASHINGTON STOVE WORKS
EVERETT, WASHINGTON

Chimney Fires

It is necessary that you clean your chimney regularly to prevent a chimney fire. Check frequently to see how quickly creosote is being deposited. You can do the cleaning yourself with a bag of straw and rocks suspended in the chimney or you can hire a chimney sweep. Remember to close off the fireplace opening before you begin any cleaning task.

If your wood-burning equipment is properly installed and well maintained, a chimney fire should not cause any serious damage. In fact, some homeowners regularly start fires in their chimneys to burn out the creosote deposits. This cleaning method is not recommended, because the high burning temperatures wear out the chimney and add to the risk of a house fire.

A chimney fire usually starts when the stove or fireplace is overstoked, thereby igniting the combustible deposits in the stovepiping or chimney. If your system is fairly clean the flames should die down shortly. Otherwise, call the fire department. The greatest hazard with a chimney fire is flying sparks and embers which may ignite your roof or a nearby combustible surface.

Heating with Your Fireplace

A conventional fireplace is an inefficient space heater for three reasons:

1. The air to feed the fire is drawn into the house through building cracks causing cold drafts.
2. The fire radiates little heat into the room and sends 85 percent of its heat up the chimney.
3. The heated air from your conventional heating system will also be drawn up the fireplace flue.

If you want to heat with an existing fireplace, limit its use to the milder spring and fall weather when your central heating is not in operation. The following suggestions and modifications will help improve the efficiency of your fireplace.

☐ When you are not using the fireplace, close off the hearth opening. Install a tight-fitting glass screen or simply cut an insulating noncombustible material to fit in the opening.
☐ For safety, use a firescreen whenever you use your fireplace. A glass screen with air inlets can reduce draft and help control the fire.
☐ Check the damper in your chimney. If there isn't one, or it isn't

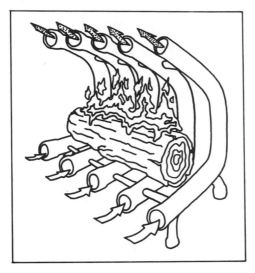

59. A tube grate will increase the heat output of your fireplace. The room air is drawn into the tubes either by convection or an electric blower. The warm air is forced through the tubes and back into the room.

working, have one installed. Close the damper whenever your chimney is not being used.

☐ New grate designs boost the efficiency of an open fire. A tube grate bent into a C heats the air passing through. Other designs radiate the heat of the burning logs into the room. The different configurations have their own advantages which may be inspiration for the clever do-it-yourselfer.

☐ Route outside air to the firebox through ducts or floor registers regulated with dampers. This modification may require professional help. It will minimize the amount of warm room air consumed by the fire and reduce cold drafts.

☐ Install a double-walled metal box to fit into your fireplace opening, usually called a prefabricated fireplace. Air can be circulated by convection or blowers through the walls and returned heated to the room. Prefab fireplaces are usually custom-made and can be designed to heat water as well. A good unit is almost as efficient as an airtight stove.

☐ Consider closing up your fireplace opening and connecting an airtight stove to your chimney.

Wood-Burning Stoves

Purchasing the right stove for your home depends on many diverse conditions. Consider the local climate, the type of wood available, the size and insulation of your home, and the existing chimney capacity. Usually, a local expert can give you the kind of advice you need; try an established hardware store or a wood-burning neighbor.

The design of wood-burning stoves has changed over the years with manufacturers producing more sophisticated and efficient models. A new stove costs around two hundred dollars with the better models costing six hundred to eight hundred dollars. Secondhand stoves can be less expensive, depending on the decorative trim, but usually require repairs. All good wood-burning stoves are in heavy demand, so expect to wait a few months for your choice.

For home heating, you'll want an efficient and airtight stove, one that gives maximum heat for minimum fuel and trouble. Buy from a reputable dealer and check for availability of parts.

Types of Stoves

Radiant Stove. A radiant stove transfers its heat to surrounding objects mostly by radiation but also by convection. Most models are airtight (air enters only through special inlets) with an energy efficiency of about 60 percent. Radiant stoves include cookstoves, space heaters, or combination units.

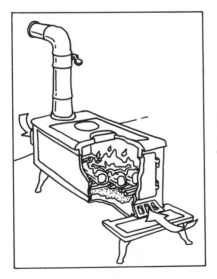

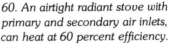
60. An airtight radiant stove with primary and secondary air inlets, can heat at 60 percent efficiency.

Circulating Stove. Circulating stoves are basically radiating stoves with an external shell or jacket enclosing the firebox. Air is circulated through this hollow space either by convention or fans and expelled into the room. The exterior surface of a circulating stove does not get as hot as

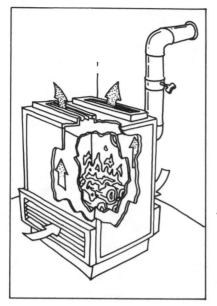

61. An airtight circulating stove warms the air as it is drawn by convection currents through the hollow space between the combustion chamber and the stove jacket. Some circulating stoves use blower units for better heat distribution.

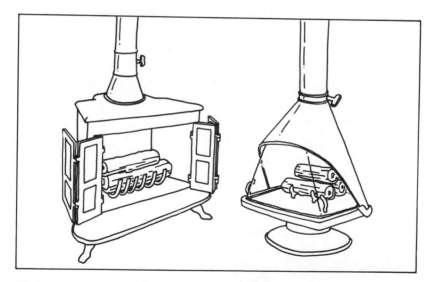

62. The above stoves, left, a Franklin model and, right, an open hearth with a metal hood are free-standing fireplaces. Unless airtight with closed doors, these models are relatively inefficient.

the radiant type because over half their heat output is transferred to the air. They are usually preferred by families with small children in the house.

Freestanding Fireplace. Both Franklin and hooded stoves have exposed fires. Unless tight-fitting doors can close off the opening to the fire, these stoves are much less efficient than the radiant or circulating types. Do not consider buying or installing a freestanding fireplace if you want a full-time heating unit.

63. A freestanding fireplace with sealed cast-iron construction and firebrick lining can double as an airtight stove with the doors closed.

Stove Characteristics

When shopping for a wood-burning stove, look for these characteristics:

Airtight Stove.	Allows oxygen to enter only through air inlets; puts out controlled heat; achieves low-firing rate and long burn.

139

Air Inlets. Primary and secondary air inlets are necessary for complete combustion of fuel; thermostatically controlled air inlet eliminates need for manual control.

Combustion Chamber. Same term as firebox—where wood is burned; stove may have one or two combustion chambers; chambers should be insulated with firebrick or metal liners to inhibit corrosion and prevent hotspots; liners promote high interior temperature for combustion of volatile gases.

Internal Baffling. Creates interior smoke path which increases heat transfer; if no interior baffling, smoke chamber can be installed.

Materials. Should be quality cast-iron or continuous-weld sheet steel; look for tight-fitting doors and well-sealed seams.

Fuel Capacity. Should be large enough for overnight fire with available wood.

Door. Must be big enough for easy loading.

Damper. Rotating plate for draft control; integral to top-loading stove for refueling; if no damper in stove, install just above flue collar.

Ash Drawer. Located under grate, makes ash removal easier.

64. All wood-burning stoves should have a damper (A). In a leaky stove, the damper will help control excessive oxygen intake. The damper should be closed when the stove is not in use to prevent cold outside air from filling the stove and chilling the room.

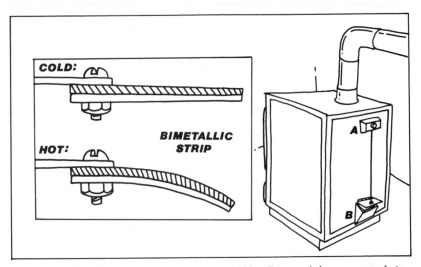

65. A stove with an automatic thermostat (A) will control the amount of air entering the combustion chamber, (B) without manual adjustment: A metal with a higher rate of expansion is bonded on top of another. As the strip is heated, the upper metal expands forcing the strip to bend downward and close the air inlet.

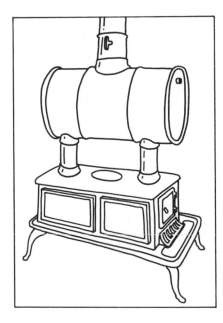

66. A wood stove without internal baffling can be modified by adding an oil barrel mounting. This "smoke chamber" provides extra surface for radiating heat into the room.

Location and Installation

Locating your stove in the center of your home will optimize its heating potential. Of course, an existing chimney and the layout of your home will determine the installation. Do not locate the stove in your basement.

Maximizing the air flow between rooms will improve the heating effects of your stove. Registers or thin openings at the top and bottom of walls and through ceilings will keep heated air moving.

It is absolutely necessary that you install your stove and its connecting piping according to local fire codes. Consult your fire department for the minimum clearances necessary.

Wood-Burning Furnaces

A wood-burning furnace is basically an oversized circulating stove ducted to deliver the heated air throughout the house. It is similar to an oil or gas furnace with a blower, air filter, heat exchanger, and thermostat. It can be installed as a dual unit (with a built-in oil backup system) or it can be synchronized with your present furnace. Wood-burning boilers are also available for central steam heating. Either unit can be modified to heat your domestic water supply.

Further Reading

1. Jay Shelton and Andrew B. Shapiro, *The Woodburners Encyclopedia,* Waitsfield, Vermont, Vermont Crossroads Press, 1976.

A useful catalogue of wood-burning equipment for comparison of various dimensions, materials, and features. Reference to this book may simplify your search for an appropriate stove or furnace for your home. Also comprehensive wood-burning background and techniques.

2. The National Fire Protection Association has published three booklets which cover safe installation of stoves, chimney connectors, and chimneys. To obtain these specifications write to: NFPA, 470 Atlantic Avenue, Boston, Mass. 02210.

The booklets are: *Using Coal and Wood Stoves Safely, Chimneys, Fireplaces and Vents,* and *Heat-Producing Appliance Clearances.*

WIND POWER

Although using the wind as an alternative source of energy is not yet financially or technologically feasible for most American homeowners, now is the time to get acquainted with the enormous potential for generating your own electricity with wind power, and to learn what is available and what it costs.

Electricity is generated on a large scale by utility companies through the combustion of fossil fuels and hydroelectric and nuclear generators. Each of these methods is becoming more costly each year in terms of money and environmental damage. At the same time the commercial development of residential wind generators is moving ahead. Reliable, cost-effective machinery will soon produce electricity from the inexhaustible, nonpolluting power of the wind.

When you are plugged into a giant utility company, electricity seems to be miraculously drawn out of the wall socket. It is therefore quite easy to remain completely detached and not really question the source or the immediate individual and community costs in terms of dollars and cents and ecological sacrifice.

We pay for electricity by the unit or kwh (kilowatt hours). The average American household buys 550 kwh each month at a price between 4¢ and 10¢ per kwh. Right now wind-generated electricity can be produced for about 15¢ per kwh. Considering the rapidly escalating price of utility-generated electricity, the gap in price is steadily closing.

A wind generator is an expensive and complex machine. To satisfy all of your electric needs would require an investment of at least fifteen thousand dollars and it is still necessary to consider wind energy as a *supplement* rather than a total replacement for conventional energy sources. Of course, if you are planning a new home miles away from the local power lines, the connection with the utility company can cost thousands of dollars. In determining whether it is cost-effective for you to invest in your own wind energy system, you should deduct this high hook-up cost from the investment in your own wind energy system.

To determine the size and cost of the wind machine which might best suit your needs and to determine whether the expense is worth it: take a few minutes to figure out your monthly electrical consumption. You can do this by following the procedure in Chapter 4. If you are serious about investigating wind power, you must carefully estimate the amount of wind available at your site.

Wind speeds of 12 miles per hour are adequate—you don't necessarily need fifty cleared acres on a windswept plain. The average wind speed at 40 feet above your backyard may be sufficient. Don't rely on Weather Bureau records alone. They will provide average monthly wind speed and direction in your area, but the microclimatic forces of nature defy such generalizations. It is necessary that you do your own readings at your site.

The most accurate method of wind reading is to buy an anenometer (wind gauge) and mount it on your rooftop TV antenna. You should take several readings every day at the same hour for several months. In fact, the longer the observation period the more accurate your monthly average wind speed estimates will be.

If the test results show that there is a 10 mph wind average for two or three days a week, then you have adequate wind speed to consider a limited wind system at your site. Now is the time to check your findings with the U. S. Weather Bureau, Federal Building, Asheville, N. C. 28801. Their records over a fifty-year period should confirm that your testing period was not a gross aberration of the long-term conditions. Also, you will notice that your data is made up of many low wind readings and a few high ones to yield a 10 mph average. Speeds below 6 mph are unusable, but those between 12 and 25 mph will provide good power conversion.

In your record of wind-speed observations be sure to note the longest periods without wind. This figure will help you estimate storage needs and backup system requirements.

Take your average monthly wind speed and read down Chart 9 until you find your average monthly kwh average. The corresponding number on the left hand column notes the nominal output rating of a wind generator in kwh. This is the capacity of the machine you need.

If your average monthly household electrical demand is 500 kwh and your average monthly wind speed is 10 mph, then read down to 550 kwh and discover that you need a wind generator rated at 10,000 watts. The extra 50 kwh per month will compensate for any power lost in storage. But there are no commercially available residential wind plants rated as high as 10,000 watts. You could install two 6,000-watt wind plants at an approximate cost of twenty thousand dollars. The length of time it would take to earn back this investment depends on your local cost of electricity.

Now take another look at your own electricity usage. Separate your requirements into categories of "Essential Use" and "Convenience."

Refer to the chapter on Household Appliances to determine how to conserve on electric consumption. Perhaps you will find that with a lower appliance demand you can make a cost-effective balance using a less expensive wind system in conjunction with your conventionally supplied electricity.

In fact, a great opportunity for wind-generated electricity exists in working directly with the utility companies. There are wind systems available today which can tie into a utility power grid. The Gemini system is capable of supplying its excess power into an existing utility network. Each homeowner then becomes part supplier and part consumer. This also greatly reduces the cost of a wind system by eliminating the need for storage facilities and a separate backup component.

Several innovators around the country have challenged the utility companies to cooperate on this venture. New York State has ruled that Con Edison must participate in this way. The outcome of the other litigations now in process will greatly affect the widespread use of wind power. The economic issues at stake are complex. The wind power supporters want to sell their power to the utilities at the same price the utilities charge. The utilities companies obviously want to buy it at wholesale prices. Clearly a broad-based equitable agreement will benefit each consumer and promote the national goals of energy conservation.

--------------------------------Chart 9--------------------------------

Average Monthly Output in Kilowatt-Hours

Nominal Output Rating of Generator in Watts	Average Monthly Wind Speed in MPH					
	6	8	10	12	14	16
50	1.4	3	5	7	9	10
100	3	5	8	11	13	15
250	6	12	18	24	29	32
500	12	24	35	46	55	62
1,000	22	45	65	86	104	120
2,000	40	80	120	160	200	235
4,000	75	150	230	310	390	460
6,000	115	230	350	470	590	710
8,000	150	300	450	600	750	900
10,000	185	370	550	730	910	1,090
12,000	215	430	650	870	1,090	1,310

Wind-Generating Systems

The idea of harnessing the wind for power conjures up the vision of a windmill. At one time there were wind pumps on farms throughout the American prairies, primarily used to pump water, but with the advent of the Rural Electric Agency in the 1950s, these became obsolete. Now once again the individual homeowner may look to the wind to help solve his energy burden.

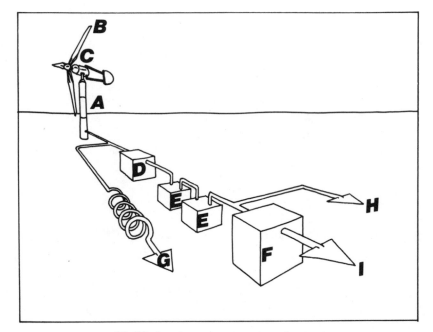

67. Wind system components and output.
(A) tower
(B) propellor
(C) generator
(D) voltage regulator
(E) storage batteries
(F) power converter
(G) resistance heating for water heating
(H) DC power for lights, tools and DC appliances
(I) AC power for major appliances, radio, TV

Components of a Wind Generator

The basic wind system will have the following components:

☐ Generator and propellor or rotor
☐ A tower to locate the generator
☐ A storage system of lead-acid batteries
☐ Power converter
☐ Backup system

The Tower

☐ When you consider the tower construction be sure to account for the structural requirements of the most severe wind and hazardous weather conditions. You have to mount the propellor at least 15 feet above any obstruction within a 400-foot radius. The tower is often 40 to 60 feet high, in order to expose the propellor to the maximum available winds. (Wind speeds are between 25 and 50 percent greater at 30 feet above the ground than at ground level.) The power from the wind is proportional to the cube of the windspeed. So if the wind speed is doubled you will get eight times as much power. Every extra mph makes a big difference.

Guyed Towers. Guyed towers are essentially the same as those used for radio transmitters. Most of their stability comes from the wire cables anchored to the ground. Their prices are very low compared to alternatives in prefabricated towers. A 30-foot guyed tower without top section may cost under four hundred dollars and under seven hundred dollars for a 60-foot model.

Post Towers. The three- or four-post tower is what you've probably seen supporting typical American family wind pumps. The base is sturdy and self-supporting. Since it requires a lot of materials, it is more expensive to build or purchase. It is possible to purchase an old tower in good shape, but be sure it is bolted and not riveted, because it will have to be disassembled and reconstructed at your new site.

Propellors (Rotors)

A fundamental principle of wind generator design is that the power from the wind is proportional to the square of the diameter of the propellor; in other words, doubling the diameter of the propellor will increase the output by a factor of four.

Chart 10 shows this relationship. An 8-foot-diameter propellor operating in a 10 mph wind can produce 75 watts while a 16-foot-diameter propellor operating at 10 mph produces 300 watts.

147

————————————————Chart 10————————————————

Windmill Power Output in Watts

assuming $P = (K \cdot A \cdot V^3) \cdot (.5926) \cdot (.70) \cdot (.70)$

Propeller Diameter in Feet	Wind Velocity in MPH					
	5	10	15	20	25	30
2	0.6	5	16	38	73	130
4	2	19	64	150	300	520
6	5	42	140	340	660	1,150
8	10	75	260	610	1,180	2,020
10	15	120	400	950	1,840	3,180
12	21	170	540	1,360	2,660	4,600
14	29	230	735	1,850	3,620	6,250
16	40	300	1,040	2,440	4,740	8,150
18	51	375	1,320	3,060	6,000	10,350
20	60	475	1,600	3,600	7,360	12,760
22	73	580	1,940	4,350	8,900	15,420
24	86	685	2,300	5,180	10,650	18,380

Horizontal Axis Rotors. The best horizontal axis rotor will provide the most power for any given wind speed. They have one main liability: the rotor must face directly into the wind in order to function. Since wind direction is constantly changing, the horizontal axis rotor must be designed to follow this change. Usually this is accomplished by attaching a tail-vane on the rotor which applies wind force perpendicular to the axis of the rotor. Another method is to position the rotor downwind from its support tower and to cone the blades so their tips are downwind from the hub.

A spinning rotor is highly resistant to any changes in wind direction. If it is spinning at a smooth pace facing into an east wind and a gust from the south pushes on the tail vane, forcing the rotor to turn south, there is considerable strain on the blades and other parts of the structure. Also while the rotor is resisting orders from the tail vane it is indirectly facing the power of the wind.

You have the choice of a two- or three-bladed system. Although a two-bladed system will run at a slightly higher aerodynamic efficiency than a similarly designed three-bladed prop, it is seldom used with generators rated higher than 2 kw output.

148

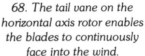

68. The tail vane on the horizontal axis rotor enables the blades to continuously face into the wind.

The three-bladed prop provides the extra starting torque necessary to overcome the difficulties found in lower winds and directional fluctuations.

Vertical Axis Rotors. Most common of the vertical axis rotors is the Savonius, developed during the 1920s. It is a simple rotor to build, using scrap metals and is ideally suited to pumping applications. A Savonius rotor can drive an electrical generator but not on a useful scale.

A very promising design developed in 1925 by G. J. M. Darrieus, has all the advantages of vertical axis design. The Darrieus can nearly match the modern high-speed rotor system in performance. The blades of this "eggbeater" rotor form a curve called a troposkein (the natural curve a flexible rope or cable will assume if its ends are tied to the ends of a spinning shaft). There are no bending stresses at high speed and they can be made lighter and more cheaply.

But the Darrieus rotor is not self-starting. There is a simple solution, however. Combining the Darrieus with a couple of self-starting Savonius rotors on the same shaft does the job. The Savonius rotors get things going and then the Darrieus rotor will take over to provide optimum performance. The Darrieus can also be started by batteries in some installations.

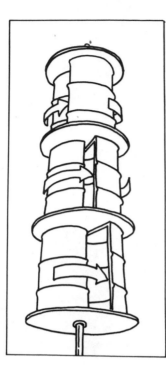

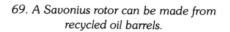
69. A Savonius rotor can be made from recycled oil barrels.

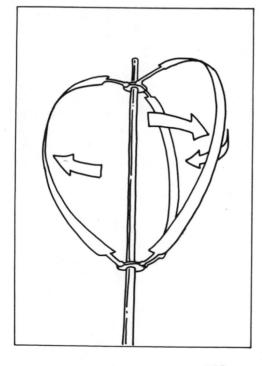

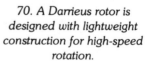
70. A Darrieus rotor is designed with lightweight construction for high-speed rotation.

Energy Storage

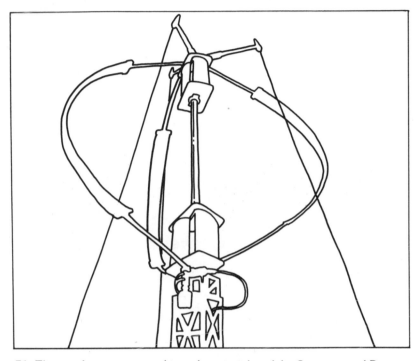

71. *This wind generator combines the principles of the Savonius and Darrieus systems.*

The major handicap of an electrical generating wind system is that the winds are not always blowing when you need them. It becomes necessary for a system to also store energy. The old standby, the battery, presently provides the cheapest, most efficient, convenient, and readily available storage option for home use. Batteries have several drawbacks, such as bulkiness, cost, and frequent maintenance. The more energy you store the longer you can do without the wind during calm spells, and the less you have to depend on a backup system. Three days' worth of storage is considered to be a workable minimum. If you can increase this to a week's worth you may be totally self-sufficient.

To determine how much storage capacity you need, take your *total kwh per month* and *divide by 30 to give the kwh per day.* Because batteries are rated in amp-hours, your total daily kwh consumption must be converted to amp-hours. You do this by dividing the watt-hours by the voltage (110 or 120) you are using.

Example:
  (1) Assume 550 kwh of electric usage per month
  (2) 18.3 kwh of electric usage per day
  (3) 54.9 kwh required storage for three days' use
  (4) A battery rated at "120 volts, 240 amps" stores 28.8 kwh.
  (5) Two such batteries will store more than three days' supply of electricity.

The batteries should be as close to the house as possible to reduce line voltage losses. They cannot deliver as well when cold and should be kept at a temperature of around 75 to 80°F. It is best to keep the batteries in the house or in a well-insulated shed adjacent to the house.

Power Convertor

Most appliances for the household use 60 cycle AC, 115 volt power supplied by the power companies. Wind systems generate DC power. They use alternators to produce AC, but this has to be converted to DC to be battery stored. A battery-powered *rotary inverter* drives an alternator which produces the 115 volt AC power you need for most appliances.

An *electronic inverter* is more expensive than rotary inverter, but it can produce static-free TV and stereo performance and it is far more efficient in turning DC to AC than a rotary inverter.

Both inverters do draw their power from your battery-stored energy, so include a switch (manual or automatic) which will turn the inverter on only when AC is needed. A surprising number of typical home loads can run directly off of 120 volt DC, such as heat resistors (irons, toasters, electric blankets, coffee makers, frying pans, hot plates). Incandescent lights and small appliances with *universal motors* can run on either AC or DC (vacuum cleaners, food mixers, sewing machines, portable hand tools).

Some appliances using only AC can be wired separately or can take an equivalent DC motor replacement. An inverter is still necessary to power refrigerators, washing machines, TVs, stereos, electric clocks, and high-intensity lights.

Auxiliary Power

For a completely reliable system you need an auxiliary engine-generator to charge the batteries during periods of inadequate winds. Even if you are willing to do without electricity occasionally you still need a unit to return the batteries to their fully charged condition periodically. Small auxiliary units usually run on gasoline, but some are available which run on LP-gas, diesel, or natural gas.

Further Reading
1. Henry Clews, *Electric Power from the Wind,* Solar Wind Co., East Holden, Maine, 1973.
2. E. W. Heronemus, *The U. S. Energy Crisis: Some Proposed Gentle Solutions,* paper presented to local sections of the American Society of Mechanical Engineers and Institute of Electrical and Electronic Engineers, Jan. 12, 1972, West Springfield, Mass.

INDEX

INDEX

Quality Nonfiction for Every Interest from PLUME

☐ **JOAN McELROY'S DOLLS' HOUSE FURNITURE BOOK by Joan McElroy.** How to make every kind of miniature "house furnishings" from early American chairs to modern sofas, refrigerators, rugs, books, even a box of chocolates. And a miniature family. Complete with color photos and drawn-to-size illustrations. (#Z5188—$6.95)

☐ **CHOW: A Cook's Tour of Military Food by Paul Dickson.** A fascinating and unique blend of more than 200 photographs, more than 100 authentic recipes, a colorful history of food and the American Armed Forces, and much, much more.
(#Z5185—$6.95)

☐ **THE BASIC BOOK OF PHOTOGRAPHY by Tom Grimm.** The complete up-to-date guide to modern photography—the most efficient equipment and the most effective techniques.
(#Z5083—$4.95)

☐ **THE BASIC DARKROOM BOOK: A Complete Guide to Processing and Printing Color and Black-and-White Photographs by Tom Grimm.** Written in clear, nonspecialized language, this authoritative book provides explanations and information on everything related to developing and printing.
(#Z5184—$7.95)

☐ **THE SHUDDER PULPS: A History of the Weird Menace Magazines of the 1930s by Robert Kenneth Jones.** This fascinating history gives you a guided tour of that golden age of ghoulish delight that produced the grisliest, goriest, most outrageous mystery-terror fiction ever sold on the American newsstand. With over 70 black and white illustrations.
(#Z5190—$4.95)

☐ **CAMERADO: HOLLYWOOD AND THE AMERICAN MAN by Donald Spoto.** A provocative study of men, movies, and the masculine image. With over 80 photographs of memorable movie scenes. (#Z5186—$4.95)

☐ **RECIPES FOR HOME REPAIR by Alvin Ubell and Sam Bittman.** At your fingertips: all the ingredients, instructions, and illustrations that make home and apartment repairs easy.
(#Z5125—$2.95)

In Canada, please add $1.00 to the price of each book.

More Quality Nonfiction from PLUME

☐ **CALIGARI'S CABINET AND OTHER GRAND ILLUSIONS: A History of Film Design by Léon Barsacq.** Foreword by René Clair. Revised and edited by Elliott Stein. A landmark study of the designers, styles, and techniques that combine to create the cinematic art . . . "A breathtakingly informative book about the movies."—*American Film.* (#Z5173—$5.95)

☐ **THE SAND ART BOOK: A Complete Course in Creating Sand Art by Suzie and Frank Green.** Written by two pioneering masters of sand art in America, this profusely illustrated book provides a complete home course that tells you everything you need to know to achieve a galaxy of your own gorgeous constructions in containers or planters.
(#Z5129—$4.95)

☐ **COUNTRY FURNITURE written and illustrated by Aldren A. Watson.** "A handsome, readable study of the early American woodcrafter and his work . . . valuable to a woodworker and entertaining for the most casual reader."—*The New York Times.* With over 300 beautiful pencil sketches.
(#Z5130—$4.95)

☐ **MAGIC: The Great Illusions Revealed and Explained by David H. Charney.** For everyone who has ever been held spellbound by an illusionist, and for anyone who wishes to be one, here is the book that will explain at last how the most astounding triumphs in the art of illusion are accomplished. With over 100 vintage illustrations. (#Z5131—$3.95)

☐ **THE CHESS TUTOR: Elements of Combinations by Leslie H. Ault.** Winning combinations as they are played by the masters—Fischer, Karpov, Spassky and others—for beginner and intermediate chess players. "A useful contribution to chess teaching."—*Library Journal* (#Z5132—$4.95)

In Canada, please add $1.00 to the price of each book.

THE NEW AMERICAN LIBRARY, INC.
P.O. Box 999, Bergenfield, New Jersey 07621
Please send me the PLUME BOOKS I have checked above. I am enclosing $_____(please add 75¢ to this order to cover postage and handling). Send check or money order—no cash or C.O.D.'s. Prices and numbers are subject to change without notice.

Name_____

Address_____

City_____State_____Zip Code_____

Allow at least 4 weeks for delivery
This offer is subject to withdrawal without notice.